GW00746298

MINISTER MATTHEW SMITH

ENTRANCEMENT

A Theoretical and Practical Manual

by

Minister Matthew Smith

Sue

[signature]

" _Today is only Important_ "

First published in 2011 by
SPIRITUS PUBLICATIONS
www.ministermatthewsmith.co.uk

ISBN 9780956960108

Printed and bound in Great Britain by
CPI Antony Rowe, Chippenham and Eastbourne

Dedicated To All Spirit Who Share Their Light

"There is always a purpose"

Ask yourself the following:

1. *Why are you impressed to investigate this form of phenomena?*

2. *Are you prepared for many hours of sitting without any seemingly results?*

3. *What is your intent?*

4. *Do you understand the levels of altered states?*

5. *Are you really willing to allow the spirit world to guide you?*

If you are, then read on.

CONTENTS

FORWARD

Whilst sitting in the power one day, my spirit helper said he had been asked to dictate this forward on behalf of those who work in the stages of entrancement from the Spirit World. They have a tremendous need for us to understand the mechanics and see it from their perspective.

We are a great army of spiritual activists trying to impinge upon mans mind the awakening of his spiritual essence.

The process is complex but the work is meaningful even if it only touches one soul and manifests a change in their thoughts processes. Our work is then allowing the individual an opportunity to reassess and see the other side to the coin of life. You are spirit now and when you allow the divine essence within you to rise to the surface all thoughts of a selfish desire are swept away. You will think and act in a spiritual sense, life will not change but the manner in which you interact will. Consequently what was seemingly a trial will become an opportunity for the soul's progression.

Co-operation is the law we work with. We have to change our own spirit vibration thus enabling the minds of incarnate and discarnate to fuse. This is not an easy exercise but is currently necessary to fulfil the obligation. As we learn and the process becomes more refined for the future generations this may change. When we see the opportunity arise to inspire it gladdens our spirit, for it is far better to strive forward together than to walk alone. Does not the music of a choir have more strength than one single voice? Is it not the combination of voices working in harmony which transcends a single solitary note? When the process has been accomplished our thoughts can be interacted with your own Similar to a choir in harmony. Each will vary for such is the pathway.

Please understand we are there to help not to hinder. We cannot interfere with your own life's lessons but are on hand to inspire your spirit accordingly. Our biggest obstacle to climb is to get you to be still. This is because the senses you possess are stimulated by and through your physical means; the food you eat, the physical surroundings, the hearing and touch all have a physical response. Therefore, to allow your mind to be clothed in a garment of peace is difficult because of those physical stimulants which you are accustomed to.

However, as part of that spiritual army our cause is not war but awakening the reality of you. Remember we work in many different ways; we have to because of the varied modes and forms which we can interact. Once you have accomplished a degree of stillness we see a window of opportunity to blend. Rather like a thread of thought where we can weave a pattern of hope to those who are willing to listen and receive. Once the thread is broken we have to redefine the power through the vibrations and conditions created.

You are reading these words because you have been impressed to do so. You may not know the source of your inspiration but that matters not. In time you may, but everything depends on your perception, which dictates our ability to overcome your logical mind.

Time means nothing in the great scheme and when we blend and work with a medium a process of learning is acquired. We are continually endeavouring to refine the process.

On behalf of the countless souls who work in this manner thank you for giving us the opportunity to shed light where there is darkness, bringing hope to a heart in despair and encouragement to the oppressed.

Suggestion: Meditate on these thoughts and see what you are inspired with.

Dictated in Southampton on March 19th 2008

CHAPTER 1

Step One

"What is more important than knowledge?" asked the mind.

 "Caring and seeing with the heart" said the soul.

Author unknown

The purpose of this book is to help you understand the theoretical and practical elements of entrancement within the stages of mediumship.

It is hoped that following your investigation, the aspects of entrancement will be clearer in your own mind, and consequently will enhance whatever faculty of mediumship the spirit world influences you with.

The techniques and theory offered in this book are primarily aimed at the student who is being impressed to sit for deeper stages of entrancement or wishes to research its value. We must however embrace the reality that **all** mediumship requires both the medium and discarnate power to adjust their level of awareness. Consequently, wherever you are on the pathway of mediumship I hope this book will give you more insight into the naturalness of your spiritual gift and the knowledge gained will help you to dispel myths and superstition. If in the process the experience helps you to think more deeply on your aspirations and enables those from the other world to accomplish the divine mission then everything has been worthwhile.

I have studied the topic over many years and write as an experienced trance medium. I do understand the complexities of this form of mediumship and the difficulties encountered on the pathway for both sides of life. Everything you read in this book is based upon personal experience. I had to learn the hard way – trial and error. The learning process is still on going for both sides. It never ends, like life.

I came into Spiritualism in the late 1970's. At that time the teaching of mediumship was totally different to today 2007.Then, you were just left to "get on with it" I was fortunate to receive most of my mediumistic training through the renowned Arthur Findlay College Stansted Hall Essex. UK. I did experience many of the great mediums of the twentieth century who were coming to the close of their working life. They were all a source of inspiration. However, and I mean this most kindly they were not all skilled teachers. I have come to the conclusion that some were not interested in the mechanics they just did it! That philosophy certainly did not have a detrimental effect on the process. We sat and listened to lecture after lecture on the spiritual implications of mediumship, awareness and allied topics. The scientific element was embraced which we seem to have lost in recent years. So the theory was rarely applied in a practical sense at the college. When I recollect, that process was right at that time. We, as students, accepted it and that's how it was. The **spiritual** aspect was encouraged, as was our motivation.

What I embraced at the college I was able to take back into the local Spiritualist church "Southampton Bitterne SNU" UK. After a period of time I was invited to sit in a general development circle in the church and very soon the personality of one of my helpers became apparent. The circle leader was a very astute medium whose awareness was extremely heightened but she did not work in the deeper entranced states. I needed more explanation in what was happening, but it was not being given. I left the circle and was invited to sit with another medium in the city. It was very frustrating as an opportunity had been provided and yet had to change. The healing leader at Bitterne invited me to join the healing team, which I did and served in that capacity for approximately 2 years. My material work meant I was not there every week, but I can now see that was another aspect of unfoldment.

I remember posing the question to spirit "Why did you lead me to the circle if it was not right?" I was told, "It was just a stepping-stone". Leaving was a very clear indication of blind faith in action on my part. These tests of faith are very important along the pathway and highlight the need for openness and willingness to listen to the "inner voice" on the trainee's part. When the second medium, Mrs Dori Morey invited me to join her circle it was a TRANCE CIRCLE. She was the medium and I sat with her for a period of about 3 years on a regular basis. After some time the spirit operators who worked with her suggested the circle sat for my own unfoldment, which we did. That particular house was used as a healing sanctuary as the owners were healers in the city. Experience has since shown me that the healing state is also passive in operation and environmental conditions created in that home were ideal for the mediumship to unfold.

We changed location when I bought my first flat and I had a room that was used just for this purpose. Throughout this time other people were led to us who voluntarily offered to sit and help. At no point was anyone asked or people interviewed as potential sitters, every aspect was spirit inspired. I can't remember how many sacrificed their time but sincere appreciation to each and every one of them has already been recorded.

Whilst writing this it is stirring up those memories of the generosity of spirit which people gave so freely. I never stopped to consider the complexities and preparation that is required for the process. I could not even begin to comprehend. It is true to say the arrogance of youth had a lot to answer for at the beginning of the pathway. I was only 20 and not many 20-year-old boys at that time were investigating entranced states within mediumship! Other states of ecstasy may have been on their minds but these would not have been spiritually induced but physically desired!

I continued to attend the Arthur Findlay College and the mediumship of the late President and Minister of the Spiritualists National Union Gordon Higginson had a great impact on my unfoldment.

The awareness shifted away from the inspired speaking, overshadowing etc. and the emphasis was on the active side of communication. Eventually I started to serve churches as a speaker working in tandem with a demonstrator and then started taking services on my own. For many years I served in excess of 200 Spiritualists' National Union Churches/Centres, Greater World and Independent churches in the UK and overseas. This is where I learnt the craft. It's rather like when you learn to drive. Whilst your instructor is there you don't really operate the vehicle yourself but when you pass your test that's when you learn! I continued to sit every day in the power and that link between the mind, body and spirit strengthened. I might add the discipline of sitting is extremely important and even after all these years I still sit on a daily basis. Consider the athlete. They have to go to the gym to follow a training pattern, which enables them to run the race, swim etc. The body is strengthened and the race can be accomplished. Mediumship is no different. Rather than visit the gym, our "workout" is sitting in the power, which strengthens our inner power and brings a closer blending of minds from the spirit world that have been assigned to work with us.

It was approximately ten years later that the feelings of demonstrating the deeper entranced states manifested along with an invitation to be a tutor at the "Arthur Findlay College" along with the experience gained on the platform as a philosophical and evidential medium.

I mention this brief outline to give you a clearer understanding of my background.

Now, as a teaching medium, I am very careful not to teach the naturalness out of the student. My style of teaching is not exactly "get on with it" but I do allow the student to come to his or her own conclusions. I offer impartial advice when asked but I never tell a student what they should do, I suggest. I feel if I tell them what to do it is denying them the rich opportunities for experience. We never learn from others mistakes because we did not live the reality. I have seen too many novice mediums being dissuaded at the hand of a teacher and being destroyed in the process. As a spiritual teacher I use my perception based on what I see, and who are we to say "you should do this" or "it can only work this way" As a student you have questions and you need to know, but please listen more to those from the other side of life who have you in their care. Remember the great mediums of the past all had a similar story to tell; it was their guides/inspirers who taught them. The medium that helped them from this side of life was merely a catalyst for the flower to unfold. As our perception is based in the here and now only those who have you in their care can with co -operation work towards your full potential.

Even from this book, if something does not feel right don't accept it. There is a Chinese proverb, which says: "A teacher can open the door but the student has to walk through it" When the step is taken of course it is frightening but that is the flip side to adventure. The one is the cause that leads to the effect. Broaden your own inner vision, if you rely too much on others opinions in can cloud your judgement and give you false if not deluded hope.

Your mediumship must not function in a robotic manner or be stylised by your teacher. I have witnessed this adoration from many students. Whilst it may appear to be complementary in action the student is not allowing his or her own spirit to shine. Remember, your spirit is part of the process and denying that aspect will hamper the progression in the long term. Please do not compare your progression or wish to be like anyone else. You are who you are not who you want to be.

You have already read the word unfoldment as opposed to development; the reason for this is simple. Some years ago I was asked by my spirit teachers to introduce the word unfoldment, as it was more conducive in the process of mediumistic communication as it was explained, "How can you develop something that you naturally have?"

Also, the journey is never ending and the word development implies an end product. It was also voiced "the faculty of mediumship is like a flower, very delicate in parts, blossoms, and has its season, returns to the source to come back again". If you are on this pathway you may already recognise that point. How many times have you come to a spiritual standstill wondering if you have been deserted by the spirit source? Then there is a change in the process when the flower blossoms again. Our mediumship is very like nature; in its powers there is a process of unfoldment and beauty. It must also be recognised that our physical life is amplification of our mediumship and vice versa. If we have had certain experiences in life the spirit people recognise this and we find ourselves helping others in similar situations. I believe this is based upon a heightened empathy and endorses the intelligence of the other world that seems to engineer the opportunity of service.

I have already stated that all types of spiritual mediumship require the medium to be able to achieve various levels of altered states of consciousness in order to link with spirit intelligence. Having this ability does not only help to accelerate the unfoldment, it strengthens the mediums link with the spirit world and defines the mediumship as spiritual as opposed to psychic. The psychic powers alone, although to some beneficial, are not manifestations of the God power with spirit intelligence. These powers are coming from the individual's own spirit and are merely "tapping into" the sitter's own energy field. When this is in operation there won't be any evidence of other spirit minds influencing the sitting/demonstration. This aspect confuses a lot of people, as the public don't realise the difference. Mediumship is induced through the medium by the God power and demonstrates through various mediumistic disciplines the "continuity of life" Psychic powers when correctly understood deal purely with the mundane of this world and do not offer any evidence of that continuity.

This leads us to the understanding of destiny. I believe we are all born with a certain pathway to accomplish; we also have freewill in the process. If everything in life were handed to us on a plate how would we learn? Also, if we are going to work as mediums the spirit powers will guide us throughout the process, as that is part of the journey for all concerned. Whether we follow that guidance or not is our choice. Some years ago the spirits who work with me said, "Destiny may be written but your desires manifest the reality" Worth thinking about!

The physical body is an amazing piece of machinery. The mind however is even more amazing. Science shows us that when a person reaches a certain age of maturity the physical body stops growing. The "mind" however continues to flourish and broaden with all the experiences and rich tapestry of life.

We know that the mind has three levels the *conscious, subconscious* and the *unconscious.*

Conscious Mind

All is recognised and reasoned in this waking state. The sensory organs respond through the brain and nervous system respectively. The mental receptivity is dependent on the individual's education and physical environment. We won't however whilst conscious be totally aware of everything which is around us as these physical senses have their restrictions. In his book "The Nature of Man" James F Malcolm says:

"In conscious activities, there is a rule of focal and a marginal field of awareness. Thus the mind is generally focused or concentrated on some particular object, thought, idea or activity (the focal field).

I believe that education is vital, the more knowledge the medium has acquired on the topic the more information the spirit people have to work with. In my experience I have found that knowledge feeds confidence and lessens dogmatic viewpoints. We should always be prepared to listen to other views, we may not agree fully but as spiritual beings we can agree to disagree. It is also impossible to love everyone in a spiritual sense. We can however try to understand them. The "trying" is a spiritual awakening within your own powers and gives others the same opportunity.

I did not always follow those thought patterns so I can appreciate and value those people who think differently...............been there!

Any spiritual pathway can at times appear to be lonely particularly if your family have differing views on the subject matter. This is where the balance of living in the now is extremely important. Our family must come first and we should never use our mediumship as a means of escapism from our physical responsibilities. A balance between the physical and spiritual is of paramount importance. The desire from those in the spirit world is to enhance our being not detract from the importance of the realism of the physical world. The views of those around us may differ but that is their right. If we all had the same thought processes how boring life would be. Consider, if all thoughts were individual grains of sand on a beach mankind would realise, like the sand, we are all inter-dependent. It matters not where we are on the beach for the life force of the tide is ebbing and flowing. When we allow the power (tide) to wash away fears, ignorance, and superstition we commune with that power of God, through our own spiritual divinity into the physical reality.

Sensitivity does not equate to a problem free life, far from it. In fact because of the process and our knowledge we are more aware of our thoughts and actions towards others. So, be prepared for highs and lows! At times you will feel vulnerable in your mediumship that's ok, analyse why, meditate on it and deal with it. If we don't understand ourselves how on earth can we begin to be empathic with other people? I believe that vulnerability is a process that occurs during the unfoldment of spiritual mediumship. If we concentrate on the seemingly negative traits when this happens we are denying our spirit friends the opportunity to help us and hampering that unfoldment. Remember it is a journey for all concerned. You will feel isolation at times but that is a manifestation of your own fears. Unfoldment is like climbing a ladder; will we be able to reach the top? What will happen if we fall? Is there sufficient support as we climb? If we get to the top what's there? Only experience can answer these questions as you blend with spirit and listen to your inner awareness.

Preparation is the key to success. The adage "If you fail to prepare then you will be prepared to fail" is very apt. Entrancement requires tremendous effort on the medium's mental capacity. People that say "I leave it to spirit" are very misguided. That speaks of an "anything will do attitude". Mediumship is far from that as it carries a tremendous mantle of responsibility. This is something I feel which is not discussed enough. As a medium you represent the voice of the spirit and the sitter/congregation looks to you as an example of whatever organisation. You are a reflection of that cause. Your work mirrors that which you represent.

I have noticed over the past years a great number of people not showing respect for the power. I find this very sad. Perhaps it is a reflection of our current society. Very much a have now pay later approach. This can never apply to your awareness. Mediumship is neither a commodity nor an excuse for a career change; it is a way of life. Commitment and dedication are vital ingredients as is common sense.

"God is your spiritual Father, and with the joy of the spirit your mediumship is that voice"

How does it work?

Ultimately it is the creative force/Power/Universal mind. Call this God or any other name, which you recognise, as the source of all life.

As Spiritualists' we know that a small aspect of "God" is within us; it is our own spirit self. This blends and reaches higher minds, which are working in complete harmony with the God force. This power can release humankind from negativity onto a pathway of love and wisdom. Taking mankind to higher spheres of truth and beauty. By these very actions the medium is registering a "spiritual intent" and creating a unity in thought and action. We experience a "blending of minds" to bring new hope to those who are searching for truth, healing to those who are perplexed, and knowledge based on reality for those who are lost or lonely. Any form of spiritual mediumship can create "Heaven upon Earth" when correctly understood, unfolded, and demonstrated to minds who are seeking other avenues of thought. Experience can't be taught, opportunities for its growth can. All are equal in the eyes of this creative force and although we may be born into different lifestyles and cultural backgrounds our basis of power is the same – our God given spirit. The Lord Buddha said "There are many pathways which all lead up the same mountain"

Our belief systems are merely different viewpoints from the mountain. What appeals to one's vision will not appeal to another but in reality everything is part of the same. As physical beings we can become blinkered if we allow the past to dictate the future or allow our mediumship to stagnate because we are in a comfort zone. The great philosophers and prophets of the past all came to teach the same message "tolerance" None of them came to promote themselves as a vast religious leader and when spirit minds endeavour to influence ours neither do they. If we look at the teachings of Jesus Christ he taught three basic truths in his mediumship.

A central creative force.
All men are brothers.
All life has a spiritual foundation.

When you listen to an entranced medium speaking those three aspects should be present. Jesus told the people "look to God, not to me" Society however has proven through the ages it needs a "figure head" which it can identify and reason with. But that is not necessary as all beings have spiritual potential. Otherwise society can then blame an individual if things don't go their way!

Any evolved soul who is working with a medium never asks us to "worship the messenger" but look at the simple truths contained in the message.

Scientists can measure and identify the pattern of brain waves through an electroencephalograph; however this alone does not prove an altered state of awareness, or influence by discarnate spirit intelligence. The mind is a very powerful tool and the novice medium needs to investigate fully if it is a discarnate power influencing the mind, or an overactive imagination.

However, imagination is a tool, which the spirit power also utilises to influence our perceptive states. The difficulty in the early days of sitting for any mediumistic unfoldment understands the difference. The general guide line is if there is feeling and knowledge within the words spoken then a degree of spirit suggestion is evident.

Pearl of wisdom

"It takes one step to begin a journey of a thousand miles"

CHAPTER 2

Brain Waves and Entrancement

Beta wave
The Conscious state
The "here and now"
Logic and reason

Alpha wave
Meditation
Inspiration
Creative powers
Intuitive/Psychic
Clairvoyance
Clairaudience,
Clairsentience
Telepathy
Overshadowing
Early signs of light trance state

Theta wave
A deepening of aspects in Alpha, more evident light trance and broader states of partial entrancement leading to the defined state

Delta wave
The Universal consciousness
Defined state
Sleep state
Some physical mediumship

These states of mind are only **part** of the process in entrancement.

The BETA state is the normal waking state. Within all these aspects there are levels within levels. For example if you drive a car or operate machinery you should be in a heightened state of BETA, as extra caution is required; reading a book or watching television would not require such an active role. Although the same degree of awareness is functioning in each action it will be on another receptive level within the beta state. Concentration through the logical reasoning mind, absorbing the "here and now" best describes the beta wave.

Once we begin to relax, our awareness shifts as the focus moves from the "here and now" and we enter ALPHA STATE. The marked changed in this is the loss of physical time, as the logical BETA state is lessened. The clairvoyant/clairaudient/clairsentient works in this alpha state when in communion with discarnate spirits, his/her conscious state is raised the discarnate state is lowered and the mind of the medium is held by this mental connection, hence the term "Mental Mediumship". The clairvoyant sees, clairaudient hears, clairsentient senses. These faculties function in an objective and/or subjective manner, the first being on the "outside" of the mind and the second inside the mind. For example the clairvoyant will say I SEE and some people see the spirit communicator in a solid form (objective) whilst some see images imprinted on their own mind (subjective) Working in this area of mediumship is an ACTIVE level of communion as opposed to PASSIVE which is induced in philosophy, deeper states of entrancement and spiritual healing. This active state is generally faster in its function and involves response from a recipient. It requires a highly unfolded medium to work in this manner, to listen to the mind of the communicator and not allow the recipient to feed them information or read body language.

Once phrases such as "I think" are uttered then we know the medium has left the alpha state and is using the beta state awareness as this governs the logical reasoning mind.

Consequently the link has been broken. That is why many mediums experience this problem; they don't allow their minds to be influenced **enough** by the discarnate spirit and are too much in a hurry to work with the public without correct investigation into their own power. I hear from many students the need to trust more in their receptive state but if the topic were studied correctly their mediumship would have that trust. A garden has to be prepared before the seeds can be set; your education is that preparation.

Education is the key that unlocks the door of ignorance and empowers not just the medium but also all spirit. I have heard some students say, "they need to be challenged" or have come to a course to be "stretched" That attitude I feel is very sad. The student is looking to the physical teacher for some miracle rather than allow the mediumship to unfold in its individualistic manner. This is neither a competition or requires a competitive attitude. Accept that the unfoldment takes time. If you don't give your spirit a chance to blend with your spirit team from the other world then the objective will be fruitless and the aims never reached. We are living in a very materialistic world and such is many peoples attitude today. Mediumship is not a commodity that can be bought it is an ability, which has to be nourished.

Remember, we can't work as spiritual mediums without the discarnate power, but that power can work without us if we abuse or neglect our responsibility.

Whatever area we are working with spirit naturally requires co –operation from both sides of life. Some years ago my helper said through inspirational writing:

> "You are on a pathway of unfoldment by reading these words your soul has already

touched your conscious mind. You are spirit incarnate. Now allow that seed to grow and form in your physical life. In doing so it will be as a bud and will blossom alone with a beauty, which Earth alone cannot bestow.

There will be times of frustration, apprehension and overwhelming excitement. This is part of the journey. Always remember you are linked as a spirit to the God force, you are not alone in your quest for knowledge. As you learn so do we. Those who link and try to influence your spirit do so because of one energy..............LOVE. With it there is everything, without it nothing.

All we ask is co – operation. Nothing will ever be said to harm you or any other Soul. Our purpose is service to humanity regardless of colour or creed."

He gave the name Ling Chan

The essence of those words I still refer to even after over 25 years of endeavouring to perfect the essence of entranced communication. You see we never stop learning. That is one of the jewels within Spiritualism. Our souls are ever reaching out to a higher purpose, which at times can be difficult to comprehend, but the door of experience is ever open to us.

At this juncture I need to explain the objective behind "names". In the early stages it is us who need to identify with a name/personality which the helpers give us. It is purely for the medium's gratification. We as physical beings identify with labels that are fed into our belief system from childhood. Once we leave our outer awareness in time we learn to unlearn and adapt to another reality..............the inner world of spirit. I was made aware of this point some years ago. I was ignorant, thinking I had to have a name for the helper. This was given (see previous inspirational writing). Further along the pathway I was told

> "Names to us are not important, we are known by our light which is a reflection of our desire. As we progress we lose the desire for remembering the physical life and if we gave our real name it would remind us and keep us in a reality that was as opposed to what is. Allow me to explain further. You are today the totality of you. Your life has all the experience and is encapsulated in your identity. Your physical body dies and the spirit is reborn. There will be a process of adjustment which would vary according to the life lived whilst incarnate. Once that has been dealt with the "Eternal progress" is open to you. If we stayed in a time warp how would we learn and how would we avail ourselves to the opportunities to grow, evolve, and attain further mantles of responsibility? We shed our personalities and those memories, as they are no longer important in our progressive life. It is true we do adopt some aspects when working with mediums during entrancement but you would not be able to recognise anything else as that is part of the overall understanding of those incarnate. You see we adapt, we have too. It is only when the medium is able to recognise and comprehend a thought as a reality we are able to infuse the process of thought as we wish to and not as the medium desires."

On another occasion I was told that it is a partnership of minds based upon mutual respect so when I hear people say "they are possessed" or "my guide made me do"…

Automatically I know this is NOT the suggestion of the discarnate. As this process goes totally against natural law which governs the work between the two worlds. These people believe this nonsense, which makes a mockery of the intelligence of the discarnate living mind. So much so it is built into their belief system and when a rational approach is suggested to them, they get even more entrenched in delusion.

So, what is the purpose of communication in this aspect of mediumship?

> To bring a closer blending of minds.
> To demonstrate the power and intelligence of the spirit world as a natural state.
> To spiritually uplift and enlighten the enquirer.
> To highlight a sense of purpose.
> Service to humanity.

So, let us examine the theory.

Pearl of wisdom
"Be still"

CHAPTER 3

Theory

First point
"To bring a closer blending of minds"

The entranced medium is working with a power that comprises:
A.   Their physical mind
B.   Their own spirit
C.   The discarnate team
D.   The God power

The physical mind has to be influenced via the medium through their spirit or as some people term "the higher self" (subconscious). This is the source of Inspiration, an awakening of that natural power that is within all people. Anyone who is creative has the ability to tap into this aspect. Whilst their training would not be of a "mediumistic nature" the outcome (uplift and enlighten) is similar. Of course people may or may not accept they are being inspired but does that really matter? Surely the outcome is more significant and its effect. It is not the route, which is important, but the journey that leads to the destination.

Inspiration stems from:
1.   Inner awareness
2.   A knowing
3.   A desire too

Inspirational speech
At the outset will be a combination of the medium's thought processes and their spirit inspirers. As the medium becomes more practised in the art form their awareness shifts away from the here and now and mentally enters into the power of thought transference. Public speaking is

an art form and if you have witnessed an inspirational address it is not just what is said but also the feeling behind the words.

In relationship to our "partnership of minds" however the training of the medium would obviously be different to the creative. The medium needs to use their own expansive awareness to allow the influence of the discarnate to blend, impress, and then enact the mediumistic faculty. How long is this process? It really depends on many factors in training and study. Each case has to be looked at on its own merit and lifestyle of the medium. The significance is the intent of the medium and the desire of those in spirit to work with us.

So now we have a stream of power that flows between the four aspects of physical emotional mind, incarnate spirit, discarnate team, and God power.

In the early days of unfoldment the medium's own mind will obviously dominate as the process of awakening and stimulating the spirit powers takes time. The logical mind is the most difficult to suppress as since our early years we are told to use and train the logical. When the process begins to shift, we open the subconscious mind where the spirit is more easily able to express its feelings and convey the thoughts/power. When our minds are open this naturally ignites our own perception and levels of receptivity. So if you are at the stage where the battle of logic/spirit awareness is a problem, accept the physical mind does play a part and don't accept that everything is 100% discarnate suggestion. It is not, and unless you reach the DELTA state, **never is.**

Inspirational writing
During this process keep your mind open, write, and then analyse.

Are the thoughts yours or the spirit world?
Are they a part of each other?
Or, predominantly from higher minds?

Define

Look at your circumstances; are the writings a reflection of where you are?

Is the philosophy based upon your level of awareness?

Is the phraseology and grammar the same as your normal day to day style?

If the answer is YES to any or all of the above you can conclude that there is no evidence of empowerment or higher influence. Many people unfortunately are misguided in this process and put everything written in the category of inspirational writing. Delusion is temporal, honest assessment is both progressive and attainable to minds who are seeking truth.

If the writing flows without hesitation through the medium, the grammar and terminology differ, we can conclude that there is a blending. The level of this will vary according to prevailing circumstances. I have known people who are dyslexic but when inspired are able to write freely. The discarnate mind by passes the mediums physical difficulty, which is another clear indication of discarnate intelligence.

When you read the script back how does it make you feel?
Does it make you want to question more?
Do you feel empowered?
Do you feel emotion when you read it back?

If the answer is YES, these are further indications of higher minds in communion.

At one particular funeral which I officiated at the gentleman's granddaughter had been inspired to write a piece some years previously. At that time she was 13 years of age. The piece did not come from any personal circumstances and her granddad did not die until some 9 years later. This is an excellent example how the intelligence of the spirit can function. Suffice to say the words and emotion touched everyone.

Can't you hear me calling?
Can't you hear me calling your name upon the breeze?
Can't you feel me watching
as you pray there on your knees?

Can't you sense the lightness,
as now my pain is ceased?

Can't you see the brightness
my true soul is now released.
Can't you hear me praying
that we shall meet again?

Can't you feel the moisture
as my tears touch you as rain?

Can't you sense my happiness
reaching out to you in rays?

Can't you see our memories
of oh such happy days?

Can't you smell the freshness
as each new day begins?

Can't you forget anger,
pain, anguish and my sins?

Can't you let go now
and let my soul be free?

As when we meet again my friend
my happiness you will see.

So, can't you hear me calling
your name upon the breeze?

Written by Gemma Coghe when aged 13

Here is another piece of inspired thought which was received at "The Arthur Findlay College.

Steps Towards Enlightenment
1.   Celebrate your individuality.
2.   Have an opinion but don't be opinionated.
3.   Be open to listen more and understand compassion.
4.   Don't dwell on yesterday but build on today.
5.   To be a complete being be responsible for all your mental and physical actions.
6.   The right intent manifests spiritual awakening.
7.   Live life through your eyes and not others opinions.
8.   Harmony stems from selfless attributes.
9.   Thought is man's greatest asset.
10. You can only do that which is right at that given moment within your consciousness.
11. Progression is healthy, stagnation is not.
12. No one is perfect but everyone has the potential.
13. Cultivate mindfulness towards all life.
14. Each steps leads towards eternity.
15. There are no negatives or positives, just opportunities.
16. Smiles accelerate your spirit, frowns age your skin.
17. Enemies are teachers you do not yet understand.
18. Learn, learn and learn again.
19. Don't try and change, allow change to happen.
20. Now go back to the first step.

Spirit Art
Here we see the medium being impressed to convey the communicative power through a drawing. A Spirit Artist captures the likeness of the communicator on paper. We

must question those who only draw guides unless ultimate proof can be given to substantiate their drawings. Whilst their intent may be pure do these individuals really exist or are they whisperings of an over active imagination?

Many years ago I went to such an artist who is now in spirit. I was so excited to find out about this helper she drew I got the picture framed and displayed it in my spirit room. One day a fellow healer from the church visited and on seeing the picture said, "You've got my monk"

I replied, "What do you mean"?

It transpired he went to the same artist and she drew him the same picture! I made further discreet investigations and discovered this lady had a catalogue of drawings that had been given to others. Identical Monks, Nuns, Egyptians, Chinese, and others. Some years later I was asked to work at a particular spiritualists' seminar and guess whom the spirit artist was? Yes I did see the history repeat itself through other excited students and although tempted to expose her, realised that was her pathway and spirit do have a way of showing us the truth. It's how we respond to it that dictates our spirituality. It was a learning curve.

On another occasion I was working at SNU Salisbury Meeting House. In the congregation was a man called Charlie Watkins. After the service he came up to me with a sketch of a Native American, which he had drawn whilst I was working. I thought, "Here we go again"

Some months later I had a sitting with Coral Polge at the SAGB in London. During the hour sitting she drew me three pictures one a relative and two were guides. One of which was identical to the picture Charlie drew some months previously. Imagine how I felt? I assumed when in

Salisbury I was being duped once again, but look at the skill and planning of the spirit in that co-operation of minds to show me "the reality of spirit".

The third picture was a Tibetan and it was over 12 years later before he began to work with me. I have never had a likeness of Ling Chan, I have yearned for it but I now know it is not necessary.

To find out more about Coral Polge's work her book is "The Living image"

Auragraphs are another aspect of spirit art, generally they tell a story of the sitter's life and spiritual potential. Whilst these do not offer evidence of survival the medium has had to reach a level of attunement to spirit to facilitate transmission of the relevant information.

Consider that:
A child has to be conceived
Then born
Nourished
Crawl
Toddle
Walk
Sprint
Run.

That is the process.

1.   You are impressed (conception)
2.   You investigate (being born)
3.   You sit in a circle of like minds or in your own power (nourishment)
4.   You go through the phase "is it me or is it other minds" (crawl)

5.   The powers are changing you go so far then draw
      back (toddle)

From the knowledge gained you let go more (walk)

The purpose is shown and the work is more productive
(sprint)

Total blending (run)

It really is a journey for all concerned.

The second point
***"To demonstrate the power and intelligence of the spirit
world as a natural state"***

The minds that work with us do so because of a specific
task. In the deeper states when the consciousness of the
medium is lessened the powers of perception are increased
and utilised more effectively by the discarnate spirit via
the medium. The discarnate does not lie, but the mind of
the medium can "colour" things. This is apparent when the
medium has not surrendered fully to the influence. That is
where we see the power ebbing and flowing. I asked if our
spirit friends find this frustrating but I was told that

***"We understand that this is part of the process, we can
see a greater picture and that is the vision we work
towards"***

In 2007 during a trance demonstration spirit said to the
novice mediums "Your minds to us are like cupboards
which are full of clutter. When we try to impress you we
have to work through the various thought processes you
have created before we can begin to voice ours"

This enforces the theory that not everything in the early
days is genuine but is voiced by the discarnate to enable

them to reach the required hold on the mind. Are you beginning to see a pattern emerge?

In my early days of investigation it was very difficult for my spirit friends to suppress the logical mind. I was both naturally curious and a born actor. I can honestly say in our case it took over 20 years before the eighth aspect (total blending) was expressed. But remember everyone is different as previously mentioned. We should never judge our mediumship by another's endeavours but simply allow the "partnership of minds" to unfold naturally. This cannot be forced as it is influenced by other powers, which are governed by the divine will (God). If you refer to the points already raised of the child in its development it is self-explanatory.

This power should spiritualise the way of thinking on a daily basis for the medium. I say should as free will and personal responsibility (5th Principle of National Spiritualism) are still in force. Entranced mediums are not puppets' acting inappropriately, both discipline and respect are engaged by our spirit friends.

At this juncture I need to make it very clear that entranced mediumship **is not dangerous/not detrimental to your health/and not theatrical entertainment.** There are cases of delusion, also people who are mentally ill with medically diagnosed illness, which has nothing to do with the mediumistic states mentioned. These souls need our prayers and healing support. It is not the purpose of this book to ridicule them. A very clear line needs to be drawn between the two. I mention these points as I am asked frequently by people who have seen the so called "entranced mediums" who unfortunately feed these trains of thought by some very bizarre behaviour.

Entranced mental mediumship does not require sitting in the dark/red light/spirit cabinets/ or any other tool that could create illusion. The spirit world requires an open mind that is willing to experiment. **If** the entranced state should lead to **physical mediumship** by those in spirit who work with you then note should be taken of their instruction accordingly. Primarily this book is covering ENTRANCED MEDIUMSHIP in the mental form as opposed to physical mediumship, which is completely different in operation, manifestation and required conditions.

Third point
"To spiritually uplift and enlighten the enquirer."

This is the key aspect. Otherwise what is the point?

History has shown us that humankind has developed a variety of belief systems. These have been demonstrated according to the culture of the individual/civilisation. Not all have been to heighten spiritual awareness and freedom of thought. For in some we see indoctrination by mankind. When loving minds in communication impresses an entranced medium, the evidence of feeling is equally important as are the words expressed. Truth can't change for it is truth. As we evolve, our understanding changes according to our soul growth. I believe this also applies in the spiritual world. I refer back to the writing "as you learn so do we"

Within the context of the spoken word there should be a perspective, which is impartial, loving, and understanding. The words will flow naturally and in many cases have a different thought pattern from that of the medium. The sitter should feel emotion of a positive nature along with the atmosphere of spirit. If they have a question in their mind and it is answered **without** giving voice, this is a very clear indication of the discarnate mind bringing enlightenment to the enquirer. There is always hope given, as opposed to criticism, love as opposed to abandonment, and freedom of thought as opposed to indoctrination. The teachings are always gentle in delivery but have a very clear thread of intelligence running through them. In my experience they always answer a question with another question!

For example: I posed the question *"Is it true that only certain people are mediums"?*

Reply, *"Are you not ALL spirit"?*

This led me to understand that EVERYONE has the potential to a greater or lesser degree as spirit incarnate (those here) for communion. If it is within the life's purpose of the individual to work mediumistically then it will unfold. God is not selective; humankind can be when they fail to listen to their own inner voice.

Do you follow the theory that your mediumship is a God given gift? Or it is an inner awareness governed by your own receptivity? Whichever thought pattern is embraced your spirit is God given and that in itself is a gift. I have come to the conclusion it is not necessary to debate the point but to rejoice in the opportunity to share that sacred power however great or small it may be at any given point.

If the entranced medium is working with "Entranced clairvoyance" the evidence needs to be excellent to demonstrate the point. The medium's mind is still by-passed as mentioned previously and the "hold" is not as deep as a more active state is required for the response of dialogue between the sitter and guide. This normally comes via the mind of the medium's helper speaking on behalf of the communicator through the medium. The medium and helper would have unfolded this method of working over a period of time to perfect the communication. So, the guide in this case acts as a "go between" for the two worlds. I have witnessed Minister and former President of "The Spiritualists' National Union" the late Gordon Higginson demonstrate such powers on numerous occasions at the Arthur Findlay College Stansted Hall Essex. Incredible attention to detail, which left the sitter in no doubt of the continued life of their loved one. More information can be found on this remarkable medium in the book "On the side of Angels" by Minister Jean Bassett obtainable from The Arthur Findlay College. I have also seen one of his guides, Cho Chow; walk the medium around the Library at the college whilst the eyes were closed and never knocking into people or talking to a wall! Always addressing and looking at people directly. I asked Mavis Pittilla OSNU who worked with Gordon extensively about this and she told me that during the early days of unfoldment the spirit team asked Gordon's sitters to organise the séance room in rows of chairs and they would induce the altered state and practice walking the medium. This would be impossible to do unless other minds are influencing the action. They obviously needed to practice this art as an extension of the powers in demonstrating trance speaking. You see, reader, if it is your destiny to do this work, then you will. The spirit people will provide all that is necessary; all we have to do is be part of the experience, listen and trust the instruction.

Fourth point
"To highlight a sense of purpose"

Everyone needs guidance in life. When in communion, these powers **always** speak in a manner which is both loving and compassionate. Their work continues in the process, bringing this awareness to those encased in a physical body, or as often referred to "matter". Of course we have trance healing mediums that transfer the power into the healing process, which still enacts "The communion of spirits and the ministry of angels" (Third Principle Of National Spiritualism)

However, no healing medium that is genuine will ever tell the patient that he/she can guarantee a cure. In my experience demonstrating trance healing I have witnessed a transformation within the patient. Trance healing works from inside the patient, it is more direct and evidential to the patient by how the power is demonstrated. It may be hot or indeed cold. I have had many patients tell me that it feels like the power is moving inside them. There have been instances where the helper has been working on the back and told the patient that a "colleague" is coming forward to work on their foot for example and describes what the problem is/was. This has never been diagnostic, as the patient already knows the condition. I have no knowledge prior to the session of the medical history. A few moments later the patient describes what is happening. I can only explain that through the blending of the medium and patient we are cocooned in a loving power. It also proves the theory that the healer does not have to touch the affected point. The power will do it automatically when we surrender to that guidance.

During a Trance Seminar in February 2008 at Kingswells in Aberdeen I was asked by the Principal Eileen Davies to give a Trance Healing demonstration to the students. My spirit team selected three patients and here are two testimonial's:

Paul/ Aberdeen

I received trance healing from Matthew on the 3rd February 2008. I have for the last few years, at times, suffered excruciating pain between my neck and shoulder due to a torn muscle suffered in sports participation.

I was immediately aware of an intense heat that came through Matthew around the area...I felt it in my body, but I was very aware of the power surrounding me. Matthew's guide also picked up on a weakness in my left ankle. Something that only I have known about since I was young. An X-Ray at the time picked up a "bubble" in my bone and I was told by the Dr that this would be the breaking point should I ever severely injure my ankle. Matthew's guide informed me that the power would be extended to my left ankle because of this. My ankle seemed then to numb for a few minutes. Before the treatment ended I was asked to place both my hands on the solar plexus whilst Matthew's guide was still working. I was told this was an experiment by the spirit and the power suddenly seemed to intensify somewhat and I was left with a sense of calm and wellbeing for most of that day.

At a residential seminar in Devon Wendy explains:

I am a large lady, and no spring chicken, with the usual aches and pains that seem to appear as you get older, but nothing specific, or so I thought!

A friend acted as chaperone as she was going to have healing after me, we were shown into a comfortable room with music playing softly in the background. Matthew explained the procedure to us, so we were prepared as neither of us had experienced Trance Healing before.

I was asked to sit in a relaxed position on a comfortable stool in front of a chair in which Matthew sat. We were quiet whilst Matthew went into a altered state of awareness, he placed his hands on m y spine and immediately I felt intense heat (like having a hot water bottle placed there) after a few minutes of this I felt quite emotional but safe. Then Matthew's guide "Ling- Chan" started to speak, he said there were problems with my right foot also my knees and another spirit doctor was coming to assist on my foot and knees. Many years ago I broke a bone in my foot and the three toes including my little toe had sort of welded themselves together over the years and although painful washing and drying them and not looking a pretty sight in sandals didn't seem too bad. Almost immediately I felt heat and movement in my foot and my little toe became flexible without pain, quite amazing. In the meantime Ling Chan is still working on the rest of me, he informed me that I had a Hiatus Hernia, which I expected and was intolerant to red meat, which I also intuitively felt. It was also suggested that I drink more water as the medication I was taking although necessary was interfering with my digestive system, he also told me a few other personal things. After approximately 30 minutes of working on my creaking body I was told that I only had to ask spirit if I needed more healing which I found to be reassuring

I felt very calm after and was given a drink of water, sat quietly whilst Matthew came out of the entranced state. My head did feel a little dizzy, but not scarily so. He explained that I may feel tired for a while and that some of the symptoms described may feel worse for a day or two.

I sat and observed my friend whilst she was having her healing and I observed Matthews face and demeanour change as he went again into the trance state as this elderly Chinese man.

For a few hours after the healing I felt fine then I suddenly felt extremely tired and retired to my bed where I slept solidly for 12 hours. Unheard of for me. My toes were the most amazing thing initially as I could move them independently and on returning home my normally sceptical husband had to admit it was something else, he was quite bemused by it!

My tummy was rough for a few days and bad heartburn. Just as suddenly it calmed right down and is now manageable. I am now listening to my body which was something I was told to do by spirit during the healing. My knees and back again felt sore for a few days. They had to get used to the fact that my toes worked again and my whole balance had to realign itself.

A few weeks have now passed and I am still progressing. Walking my lovely Springer is now a pleasure as my knees aren't so creaky and the old toes are still working well.

Spiritual healing works primarily through the auric field of the patient. Whilst this and the deeper states are both beneficial they both operate within spiritual law. Each experience and mode of working differs according to the unfoldment of healing powers and understanding the application. Sometimes this has been subtle or in certain cases more profound. As with the case of any evidential communication the way the power is received will affect the quality of evidence. Remember this is a conversation of minds. Even in the case of "Healing Mediums;" although conversation in words may not be taking place the recipient's mental attitude can still affect the outcome. Do not the spirit people tell us that the "mind is the builder"? Whilst we are working with a power that is really remarkable it is understandable that the uninitiated will have reservations. As a spiritual medium it is your job to offer assistance, to portray the power as a reality and allow the recipients to come to their own conclusions. Never be over enthusiastic but supportive and don't be so sensitive or ultra-spiritual that you have no earthly purpose! A healing medium must not guarantee to cure the patient and should always encourage the patient to use orthodox medicine as a first priority and healing as complementary. A healing channel works with the God power, they are not God!

Fifth Point
"Service to humanity"

It's never about self; it's about being self-less.

The ancient Greeks looked upon mediums as "Oracles of God" and although some of their practices today would be frowned upon it was in their understanding/belief system. The definition however is still apt in the 21st Century and history will continue to depict it so.

Let us look at the work of Mother Teresa (27th August 1910 that died on 5th September1997) as an example. She worked as a channel for the spirit in the understanding of Catholicism. Truly a source of inspiration for countless thousands and her work continues as a living testament. We must also remember that any religion is "man-made", but our spirits are "God given" and our pathway of understanding will develop according to our life's destiny. It does not matter how the power manifests, it's the service it renders. What has this got to do with entrancement I hear you say? But readers don't limit your vision purely within the confines of Spiritualism, our spirit friends don't! Once we become blinkered and dogmatic in our views, it limits the expressive source.

Entranced utterances, healings, philosophy, and evidential mediumship in Spiritualism are miniscule in comparison to the divine plan. God is not selective as already mentioned and those of us who work within the understanding of "Mental Mediumship" do not know all the answers because we don't know all the questions. Service is a never-ending pathway, so be prepared!

Mother Teresa took her inspiration from St Francis of Assisi and if you look at the spiritual implications of his prayer it will apply to each one of you today.

> Lord, make me an instrument of your peace,
> Where there is hatred, let me sow your love:
> Where there is injury, pardon:
> Where there is doubt, faith:
> Where there is despair, hope:
> Where there is darkness, light:
> And where there is sadness joy.
> O divine Master, grant that I may not
> So much seek to be consoled as to console;
> To be understood as to understand;
> To be loved as to love:
> For it is in giving that we receive;
> It is in pardoning we are pardoned;
> And it is in dying
> That we are born to eternal life.

These words were given through the inspirational state from spirit to St Francis. The Catholic Religion would have influenced his own mind as his own belief system. Hence the terminology "Lord" and "Master". However, this does not deflect from the essence of the piece and is as applicable today in any walk of life as it was when written.

Before she died Mother Teresa spoke the following words, with which I would like to conclude this chapter.

Advice for Living

People are often illogical, unreasonable, and self-centred:
Forgive them anyway.
If you are kind, people may accuse you of selfish ulterior motives:
Be kind anyway.
If you are successful you will win some false friends and true enemies
Succeed anyway.
If you are honest and frank, people may cheat you:
Be honest and frank anyway.
What you spend years building someone could destroy overnight:
Build anyway.
If you find serenity and happiness they may be jealous:
Be happy anyway.
Give the world the best you have, it may never be enough,
Give the world the best you've got anyway.
You see, in the final analysis, it's between you and God,
It was never between you and them anyway.

Pearl of wisdom
"Inner turmoil is created by lack of vision"

CHAPTER 4

Karmic Law

The word Karma means both deed/work, the results of a particular deed and the chain of causes and effects that link the various deeds together.

Karma is the accumulation of ones actions in life that is carried forward affecting your and other people's lives. The laws of Karma are principles in their own right.

They provide lessons that teach us to confront the reasons for this life. When correctly applied and understood they **should** liberate us from painful illusion that stops us from reaching our "spiritual destinies". **These are the laws of the Universe and so are applicable in all levels of consciousness.** When we begin to understand them they are liberating and give us the freedom and insight into our spiritual aspects.

Remember you are spirit first and body last and the first step in any awareness is to commune with that power which is your right.

What are they?
1. The great law.
As you sow so shall you reap.

2. The law of creation.
You attract what you are not what you want.

3. The law of humility.
What you resist persists for you.

4. The law of growth.
Wherever you go there you are.

5. The law of mirrors.
Whenever there is something wrong there is something wrong in us.

6. The law of synchronicity.
Whatever you do may be insignificant, but it's important that you do it.

7. The law of direction and motives.
You can't think of two things at the same time.

8. The law of willingness.
If you believe something to be true, then sometime in your life you must demonstrate that truth.

9. The law of be here now.
Looking back prevents us from living in the now. Old thoughts, old patterns of behaviour, old dream all prevent us from having new ideas.

10. The law of change.
The more things change the more they remain the same.

11. The law of patience and reward.
When you focus on your life good things happen.

12. The law of value and upliftment.
What you put in you get back.

All of these laws are based on spiritual and human endeavour. None are punishment but operate on a spiritual base, which manifest throughout all areas of life. They cannot be escaped or avoided. Each has a purpose for the progression of the individual and ultimately the collective mind working in perfect harmony.

Further insight on Karmic Laws.

1. Take a good look at your life in its totality today. Don't become a martyr in the process but equate what is and why. Our lives are a direct result of this law. They are a living testimony of every thought deed and action. If there are aspects which manifest emotional or physical pains, do not look to the effect but change the cause. The powers are within us it is that simple.

2. The spirit powers can only speak to us at a level we can understand. No language can be understood if it has not been lived. Consequently if we yearn for something that is outside our experience it is not real.

3. Stripping away the ego and seeing the spiritual value before anything else.

4. All things are possible.

5. Don't waste time and energy criticising others look to self-perfection.

6. All life has value and behind each experience is an opportunity for growth, nothing is mundane with spiritual intent.

7. One thought, one action one result. Two thoughts, muddled reaction no significant result.

8. By keeping a belief without breathing life into it through action is only a half-truth.

9. Living in old thought patterns create obstacles and stifle inspiration.

10. Things are not important, physical life is an illusion, perspective is the reality.

11. To expect miracles is misguided vision. Don't chase rainbows in life, make them happen.

12. A smile can create another smile negative action creates adverse reaction.

These laws are so in depth it is impossible to give full explanations in a few pages. The earnest medium will find out more and study the topic as a separate issue. Mediumship alone does not operate within these spiritual laws they govern all life and are applicable to both levels of consciousness.

If you study them they are interwoven and the great law "cause and effect" operates on a daily basis. Sometimes we as humans are so engrossed building our own "castles in the air" our focus can shift away from the original purpose and intent. That's life, it happens. It is necessary we remind ourselves of that purpose when we feel we are loosing our way on the path.

If you are struggling with any issues I would suggest you look at the given laws and see which one you feel connected with. Then, sit in the power of your own spirit and ask for further insight. Don't expect any loud voices ringing in your ears or visions of guides around the room. Be still and listen to your inner feelings, this is the voice of your own spirit. Listen to it, work with it and embrace the reality.

You see reader to be a channel for the spirit world we as mediums have to be in harmony firstly with our inner spirit power, if not how can the discarnate mind blend with us? Sometimes we do have to face issues and deal with them. Generally these "issues" are part of our life's pattern and are there for our and others progression. To deny them is to deny the bigger picture being created. Creation is perfect and if man worked more closely with the laws of the Universe the rhythm of life would be more harmonious.

Let's remember, none of us are perfect, that's why we are here!

Pearl of wisdom
"Perfection is possible once imperfection is embraced"

CHAPTER 5

The Pathway

Step 1 Meditation

This is a discipline, which is greatly misunderstood in Spiritualist education. It has nothing to do with discarnate communication. It is a tool, which helps us within the physical life and aids us in a spiritual quest.

The mind has many layers. We continually fight in adult life with the logical mind against the emotional. Do you say, "Is it me or is it spirit"? Yes? Then you know what I am referring too.

As children we naturally live with our emotions. Don't children speak and act in a spontaneous manner unless otherwise conditioned? When we reach adolescence this is drummed out of us because of hormones and peer pressure. We no longer think in total innocence, as the world around us seems to be changing. Of course it isn't we are. The emotional is being suppressed to make way for the logical. The material sense of life is becoming more realistic for survival. We start to analyse and become conditioned in the thought process. We move away from childlike ideals, as they no longer are important in our education. The physical world is now more of a reality than our emotional. We begin to look "outside" for answers and stimulation. This I believe is why today (2007) we are seeing a lot of young people dependent on drugs and alcohol, which can lead to other forms of abusive behaviour.

So it follows when people come into the awareness of "spiritual values" they do so with superstition and disbelief.

Do you remember as a child playing with that cardboard box? No longer did it hold that form, it was your shop, car, tent or some other plaything. In your imaginative mind it was real. The boxes led you to a form of entrancement and make believe. It took you on a journey into another reality. That is the key to meditation practices.

Let us embrace the fact that there are many forms of meditation practices which all play a part in their relevant religion/philosophy. What works for one individual however will not necessarily work for another. So we need to look at:
1.   The individual's background.
2.   Motivation of self.
3.   Understanding self.

With this in mind we then embrace those layers and strip away that which is logical and begin to listen again to the emotional.

It is impossible to "make your mind a blank" The brain is the hard drive of the computer (body) which functions and operates on a physical level. Like any computer it has to be programmed to act on instruction. Your thoughts are that programme.

In the beginning allow those distractive thoughts to enter the mind, deal with them then dismiss. By entering into this mental dialogue we are re-programming the layers. By answering the logical we are lessening its control and opening the doorway of the emotional self. Don't expect drastic results overnight. It takes time/discipline/and patience. Consider how long it has been for you to establish the naturalness of the logical self; we now have to unlearn to learn. As with all spiritual aspects the time span depends on you.

Some frequently asked questions on Meditation
Do you have to listen to music? No.

Do you have to sit in any specific position? No.

Do you have to sit in silence? No.

Do you need to sit for a specific time span? No.

Will any harm come to you? No.

In short, always do what feels right for you. When the process changes allow it to. Don't get into any ritualistic practices, to do so manifest routine as opposed to spontaneity.

Many years ago my spirit teachers told me "If the mind is open the spirit can sing"

In meditation the statement points to your own spirit in partnership with and through your physical self.

Some years ago a study was made at Harvard University Boston USA from a cross section of people who practiced various forms of meditation. The study concluded:

Meditation can help strengthen an individual's immune system

It can help with orthodox and complementary therapies.

Bring a sense of detachment from physical pressure.

Peace of mind and enforced mental strength.

A realisation that they were no longer alone.

It was also noted that to achieve the above the individual needs to practise on a regular basis and must focus on the positive framework of thought. It was also stated that any form of meditation is **not** an alternative to medical treatment so anyone who needs medical attention should seek it first.

Some subjects said for them after a period of time meditation became as natural as breathing.

Problems encountered
- Letting go.
- Trying too hard.
- Understanding during experience.
- Listening to others.
- Analysing.
- Mental discipline.

Solutions
- Prepare your environment.
- Acknowledge distractions.
- Accept the mind can colour.
- It's always a personal experience.
- Work through the layers.
- Focus.

Meditation can also be stimulated by active activity. Going for a walk, being in your own garden, walking by the beach. The process enables you to "switch off" from day to day stress and allow whatever atmosphere you are in to embrace your own spirit. If you are one of these people who have a "butterfly mind" then try this as an alternative.

Please also understand that meditation is not relaxation. So, if you fall asleep during meditation you are relaxing as opposed to meditating. The common problem for this is lack of focus. By focusing it keeps you in the right frame of mind and opens the doorway for your spirit to impress that mind.

Before we can continue on the pathway meditation **has** to be mastered.

Step 2 Attunement

Having mastered the art of meditation we now move into the next phase.

We have left the outer awareness and tapped into our spiritual self. The aura of the medium will become charged with spiritual thoughts through the process of suggestion. In the early stages of this awakening it is vitally important the novice medium uses discretion. As the mind can still, to a degree, manifest its desire. As the process becomes more charged however this will lessen and the attunement becomes more plausible.

Think of a radio set. Its frequency has to be adjusted to receive the signals from the radio station. If they are not correctly picked up the transmission becomes weak and some aspects are lost. That's attunement!

Your spirit is the radio station and your mind is the set. The conditions you sit in will dictate the frequency of transmission and the receptiveness its clarity. When the mind interferes the frequency becomes hazy because it has mentally hampered the chain of thought. Some students tell me that their fear is based on getting it wrong and consequently becoming delusional. I disagree with this point. My feeling is it's the fear of getting it right that hampers students. Yet they are unable to accept this truth. Why right? The human ego is such that if it succeeds on a certain level it feels it must "top it" next time. When working with the power however this is not necessary. There is a Native American saying, "You think your ego is your best friend, in fact its your worst enemy" I offer this as an explanation; you of course must come to your own conclusions.

We now see the medium's own spirit impressing the mind through the faculty of perception and suggestion.

The more attuned the medium the clearer the message relayed. Doubt is replaced with clarity and reason. This is a very clear indication that the mediums mind is being influenced by other powers, and, in deeper entrancement, higher minds. You are voluntarily taking your mind to other levels of awareness but will only receive what you are able to perceive through the transmission. That is an important point to remember.

Mediumship is like a forest; there are no straight paths!

Third step Entrancement
Discarnate powers induce the altered states of entrancement with the medium's co-operation. This only happens when the first two stages have been accomplished

and a very clear co-operation of minds has been established. The impressions are then much stronger. It has taken a considerable amount of patience and perseverance for the "spirit team" to blend with the medium and for trust to be gained by all concerned.

The next chapter deals with entranced states in more detail.

The Pathway step by step
Prayer manifests your intent into energy.
Your consciousness is raised and your team's lowered.
You then blend.
The power is transferred by spirit through you.
Train your mind to be open.

You are the medium, not a guru.

The power will endeavour to restore a balance for all concerned.

Everyone has to play his or her part in the process.

It's a team effort.

Put your total trust in that which trusts you.

Don't get into a routine.

We, and the team are always learning.

All sessions are experimental.

Nothing can be guaranteed.

Remember you are working with intelligence.

Time is not important, its use is.

You are responsible at all times.

It's a long pathway

Work in light and be enlightened.

You will have noticed I use the word entrancement as opposed to trance. The former I feel gives a clearer indication of the process. If you take out the last four letters you have entrance, which is how I see the work. A mental doorway for higher minds to impress and release mankind from the limitations and restrictions of dogma and creed. Both of which are founded upon fear and not liberal thought, which is based on reason.

Pearl of wisdom
"As spirit you are always in that presence"

CHAPTER 6

Control or Suggestion?

Spiritualism has its own language and to the uninitiated can sound rather complicated and confusing.

Within the process we are investigating the word **"control"** is often used. It refers to the discarnate mind (spirit intelligence) that is responsible from the other world for the manifestation of power through the medium. The word control however is misleading in our understanding. In our language it means "in charge of" and consequently implies the medium is not. This is incorrect. As an entranced medium YOU are responsible for the manner in which the power is portrayed. I prefer to use the word **"suggestion"** as opposed to control. The old language of stages is; light control, overshadowing, control, full control. As you read further you will note I have updated the terminology which, in my opinion, gives a clearer understanding. You see reader, as we are working with intelligence, anything that is beyond reason will not apply in the process. If as an observer we see and experience the opposite then that is a clear indication that the novice medium is working with their personal thought process, and not with the influence of higher minds. The "team" which work with the medium do so for a specific purpose/task. One individual develops a special link with the medium and here we have the true meaning of the word **guide.** This is mistakenly individualised by many novice mediums. As we live in a physical world everything is identified as male/female/belief system etc. The uneducated will naturally follow this thought process through without looking at the broader reality of "minds inspiring minds".

The aspect of trance suggestion applies from the spirit side, where a GROUP of like minds are working together with the medium. It is a team effort and not an individual pilgrimage. We also know that "minds are inspiring minds" in the process of unfoldment for all concerned (incarnate and discarnate).

So, you as the medium are in control of the suggestion that is being impressed upon your mind by many inspirers through the guide. From the spirit world that team are in control of the process. We as mediums must always be aware of moral conduct and spiritual values, which are "service to humanity regardless of colour or creed"

Facets of Entrancement

"Remember, there are levels within levels"

Inspirational Speech

ALPHA state stage 1 and 2. This is a power that can stir the soul. The medium in almost all cases will be working with their eyes open during inspiration. This helps him/her in the realisation of where they are and does not give the wrong impression to the sitters. Your own mind will play a part in the beginning before your own spirit self has been awakened. The novice will often feel a sense to speak or act in a certain manner. External thoughts when higher inspiration has been reached will flow into the mind (stage 2). These will emanate from a source beyond our comprehension but will blend with our spirit power and be relayed through the physicality of the medium. Depending on the unfoldment of the medium, sometimes the words, phrases, thought and speech pattern are similar to the mediums. Consequently doubts arise within the novice's mind during the process. We must remember that in all aspects of mediumistic unfoldment the discarnate power has no choice but use our 'mental awareness'. Therefore, particularly in the early stages, that power has to break through our consciousness and unconscious mind then learn how to influence the flow of thoughts. The group will study the mechanism of our minds. That is why we say that each time we work with spirit it is experimental. Any aspect of entrancement is extremely delicate. The novice medium needs to develop a trusting attitude towards the power, which is unfolding its awareness with us. Then, over a period of time it will be realised how the pattern changes and the inspiration becomes more powerful. It can't be done if the mind is closed and not open to experiment. The level of suggestion will dictate the essence of inspirational flow. If the medium's mind is truly entranced you will witness a natural flow and feel as an observer entranced by the power.

It does not follow that as an observer you have to be mediumistic as we are looking at mental mediumship in operation.

As a speaker, you will lose a sense of physical time, as will your listeners, because the ALPHA state is enacted. You will also have some degree of recollection of what has been said. The level of "hold" will again vary according to the level of perception and spirit suggestion from conditions created. In the early days it is a very good idea for the novice to record the session either by audio or video equipment. This will give the novice a true reflection of what has taken place. We can't always rely on friends/colleagues being realistic in assessment.

At this point I would like to explain the terminology **"hold"** When the spirit essence impresses the mind it's like a conversation that ebbs and flows. You as the medium have to believe what is being impressed; failure to do so will weaken the clarity of power. How would you feel if you were trying to speak to someone and they didn't believe you? Put yourself in the position of the spirit people. Not a nice feeling! However if you are positive in your approach then encouragement replaces doubt and strengthens the connection. The hold then allows a natural momentum to unfold.

You may, as an observer, realise that a degree of the medium's mind has coloured the conversation but don't look just at what has been said but how it was said. The power/feeling behind the words is a very clear indication in all areas of "hold". This has nothing to do with self-hypnosis in the conventional sense. The medium has raised their own consciousness and through the blending the discarnate powers have lowered theirs. To explain further the "hold" is a "meeting point" of reason and rationality. Once that thread has been broken and the medium leaves the stage of entrancement, a technique used to retrace the mental steps is to repeat what was said in the altered state, which establishes the flow once again. This of course is pointless if the dialogue has come to its natural conclusion.

Some further points to help you at this stage
- The novice medium has to be secure in the environment of sitting.
- Needs to be willing to experiment with spirit.
- To allow the spirit power to blend and medium to listen to those feelings.
- To give voice from the feelings no matter how trivial.
- To embrace errors as challenges.
- To know that the spirit can't lie, but the mind can colour.
- To know that defeat is not within the soul.
- To celebrate what has been achieved.
- To recognise progression and purpose within communication.
- To be aware, to believe, then to know.

Light Trance State Alpha Stage 3 and Theta Stage 1

The medium will still be partly conscious during the speech/experience. There may be a slight change in their personality/voice inflection/mannerisms. The discarnate team will be able to influence the medium's mind more than inspirationally because a stronger degree of blending will have taken place. The medium may or may not be working with their eyes open in this level. That depends on the medium's ability to trust.

The more we as a medium have become entranced, the less emphasis is in the here and now "BETA" state. If we were looking at someone their body language will dictate signals that will influence our mind. Therefore the closing of the eyes helps to subdue the medium's personality and detach them from the physical surroundings. In a way it desensitises the medium from the physical environment and opens a mental door for the spirit self and discarnate team to impress freely without added distractions. That is why it is important for you as a medium to have someone else looking after your welfare, particularly if you are giving public demonstrations. This, like all stages, will ebb and flow and will happen naturally. At no time during the sitting should the medium interfere with the thought flow. If they do then the link will be broken. Remember the "partnership of minds" terminology used is also a good indication as to the degree of inspired hold.

The medium will also recall either some or all the entire activity at this level.

Mental impression Alpha Stage 3

The medium will still be conscious to a degree and an extended awareness with spirit will be apparent. The level of power is the same as light trance state but rather than the power being expressed in words, the energy is used to impress the features on the medium's face and at times posture of the body. If speech is also enacted with this the medium will enter into THETA (stage 2) also for that purpose. Remember all the work is about spirit energy. If one aspect is being used to create a particular hold then the spirit team can utilise other areas of entrancement in the sitting. It sounds complicated on paper and in theoretical terms it is. The process is slow for the spirit people with the medium during the unfoldment. The end results however when the impression is **truly** evident breathes more reality into the experience. In the early stages any impressions will be exaggerated but please remember to leave the process in the hands of those who work with you. If you sit with pre-conceived ideas then the mind is not truly open. This process may not even unfold in your particular form of entrancement. As previously stated it depends on the abilities of the team, the purpose, and openness of the medium.

Quite often the uneducated confuse this mental impression with transfiguration. They are completely different. The process of mental impression is a fine blending of energy from the team, which is impregnated into the medium's aura, and then the medium's face/body is used as a mirror for that helper to impress his/her personality through the medium. The onlookers will see the result with their **own individual perception.** It must also be noted that some people will see what they want to see and can be carried away on a tide of emotion. When the physical impression has reached a level for public demonstration it is usually the guides/inspirers of the medium who utilise this form of mediumship. They will have sat with the medium over a period of time for this purpose. This is another aspect of entrancement as discussed and like other areas mentioned falls under the category of **"Mental Mediumship"** This explains that the process is through the enactment of co-operative thought from both sides of life.

Physical mediumship (Delta)

Unlike the mental impression, transfiguration is a power, which is not subtle but obvious to all who witness it irrespective of mediumistic ability. This is why it comes under the category of **physical mediumship.** Ectoplasm is formed as a mask, which is slightly in front of the medium's face and in some instances on other parts of the medium's body. It looks like a solid mist. The spirit personality then transfers their features into the mask which everyone can see. This form of mediumship will still have been unfolded over a period of time before public demonstrations. People's deceased relatives/friends will transfigure and sometimes guides/helpers. The purpose is to commune in this manner with their loved ones who are still this side of life. Completely different in its purpose and operation from the mental impression.

Many years ago I had sitting with a medium called Olive Tomlinson (now in the spirit world) who lived in Uxbridge. She was visiting Bitterne Spiritualists' Church in Southampton. In broad daylight during the sitting the face of Ling Chan transfigured and spoke to me. The content of which was personal but relative at that juncture of my life. The mask was evident and it was not my objective clairvoyance in operation. Now that instance dispels the myth that transfiguration can only happen in red light, as many people believe. I have thought on this experience long and hard and asked my spirit friends for an explanation. I was told:

"That the conditions were conducive for such mediumship and because of our pathway ahead it was necessary for the spirit people to produce these phenomena".

(Abridged explanation)

It certainly made me think and stimulated a desire to enquire further. I have a lot to thank that lady for; she played a very important role on my pathway.

Partial Trance State Theta stages 2 and 3

The medium is now less aware of the proceedings and more of the spirit mind will be evident. The topics of conversation may differ from the medium's own views. The thoughts will be more fluid in delivery. The medium's own mind will be more passive to enable this stage of entrancement. Their logical mind will be almost totally suppressed and the emotional self is heightened. There will be wisps of thoughts that the medium will recall but much less than the previous stages. From my own experience I describe this state as total surrender to the team. I don't leave the body or feel myself standing outside as an observer. Mentally I withdraw and feel very much part of the experience although as previously mentioned there is limited recall of points of conversation.

It is very difficult to explain, as each person will be different in his or her understanding. As with all aspects within Spiritualism the reality is personal journey, please remember, that is very important. Wherever you are within this process don't judge your own mediumship by others. It will weaken your perception if you do.

At this level the observer should be aware of the depth of knowledge the spirit impart. It must be outside the medium's normal understanding. The dialogue must be evidential in all aspects. If not then the state is 'self-induced' as opposed to 'spirit inspired'.

Indications of Entrancement

In the early stages very few sensations/feelings are registered by the novice medium. The most difficult hurdle is being still!

Once that hurdle has been overcome the following are indications of entranced blending

- Sensation of growing or shrinking.
- Seeing light/colour.
- Heat/Cold.
- Changes in breathing pattern.
- Pulse can become slower.
- Cobweb type feelings on face.
- Throat restrictions.
- Inability to control saliva.
- High emotion.
- Palpitations.

The medium's awareness is beginning to extend beyond their normal state of now and the sensations are emanating from their ethereal body.

These are indications through the medium's sensitivity which when unfolded could lead to the physical changes i.e.:

- Personality.
- Voice.
- Poise.
- Mannerisms.
- Idiosyncrasies.
- Different Languages.
- Differing views from those of the medium.
- The presence of spirit.

When we witness the partial/defined states of awareness, the mediums personality has changed and the spirit people are refining the blending process. As "Silver Birch" (Guide to Maurice Barbanell) said very eloquently "from spirit, through spirit, to spirit. At this juncture those observing should be aware of the presence of spirit.

Defined Trance State Delta

There would be no question in the observer's mind if this were being demonstrated. The medium would be totally unconscious and the spirit team have 100% hold on the medium's mind. At this juncture the spirit power is between the medium's ethereal body and physical body. Unlike the partial state where the process is Physical/Ethereal/Spirit.

In my experience I have not witnessed anyone at this level or practised this myself. I was asked by the team if I would co–operate to this point but refused. As a child I was epileptic and I have a fear that if I go to that level it could trigger a fit. Where is his trust I hear you say! I raise the point to illustrate that your own free will is a reality. Saying no has not hampered the work or the progressive unfoldment.

Many years ago in the early days of entrancement we are told that the Delta state was the norm. We however were not there! I can only comment from personal experience. Measuring that against the reality of today we can come to a conclusion. In another 100 years or so the process will be different again. Society will have changed; the spirit people will have had more experience through many other mediums, so we see the process continually refining. **That is spiritual mediumship when functioning with co-operation.**

You cannot measure a person's link with spirit by reading a book or listening to other people. It's about being in that power and feeling the unconditional love. It really is very humbling and enlightening.

Aspects to consider

- The states can fluctuate when a level of entrancement has been achieved.
- It is not necessary in the early stages for the medium to have their eyes closed.
- It should not be taken as fact that a stage of entrancement is demonstrated unless;

1. The power of the spirit is felt by the majority present - irrespective of their mediumistic ability.
2. That which is said has benefit, worth and meaning to those observing.
3. The thoughts offered are not dictatorial or dogmatic.
4. The experience has stimulated the observers own thoughts.

Whatever is said is always the medium's responsibility not that of the spirit world.

Pearl of wisdom
"Food may feed your body, but knowledge nourishes your spirit"

How true!

CHAPTER 7

Environmental Conditions

Sit in a manner, which is comfortable for you. Use a chair that is supportive to the body. Avoid low chairs or settees, which suggest sleep as opposed to mental exercise. Your sitters should also be seated in a similar fashion. There is a train of thought that people should sit in a circle. Personally I don't feel that is important, harmony of minds is more paramount. If your preference is to sit in that conventional way do so. Use lighting which is subdued, table lamp or similar. Preparation of the room is equally as important as to your mental openness. Conditions are more preferable if the same room can always be used and closed off before sitting. This gives the operators in spirit more opportunity to "spiritually prepare" the room. Music is also a personal choice. If desired this could be played for about one hour before sitting. If candles are being used it is not advisable to leave them unattended. It is a question of trial and error until the conditions are conducive. The ratio of sitters is obviously governed by space, use common sense. Some mediums like flowers in the room as they represent the force of nature. Perfumed flowers should be avoided. Personal preference again will dictate. Generally an atmosphere of warmth and serenity needs to be created which is welcoming and supportive. The temperature of the room should be moderate and the sitting period should be approximately one hour's duration on the same day and at the same time. Weekly sitting is preferable to fortnightly. Sitters should arrive at least 15 minutes prior and punctuality is very important. This is an appointment. Any mundane or negative conversation must be avoided prior to sitting, remember thoughts are living things!

Negativity when spoken or in thought form goes into the atmosphere. This creates a mental barrier. It was explained to me from their side such conditions are like a fog, which make their work increasingly difficult.

An opening prayer should always be spoken which invites and welcomes all present and mentally sets the "intent" for the group. At conclusion a closing prayer of thanks must be given. Before the group depart a warm drink should be given to everyone, this provides as a means for discussion for what has taken place and gives people an opportunity to share and adjust back into life.

If the sitting period is in daylight hours I would suggest that curtains/blinds be drawn. This helps to cocoon the room and help the sitters adjust and avoids any unnecessary distractions. Water must be available for all concerned should the need arise. It is advisable to place this under/by each seat as standing and breaking the chain of power is unhelpful to the spirit operators. As already mentioned the power is a very delicate thread and we need to understand its complexities. No one should leave the room before the conclusion of the sitting unless permission has been asked from the circle leader. The sitters should be wearing comfortable clothing, which is not tight or restrictive. This applies particularly to the novice medium. The wearing of any strong perfumes/colognes should be discouraged. When anyone enters a sensitive state his or her physical senses are heightened. Consequently any fragrances of a physical nature can be distracting to the awareness of the novice medium and sitters. Anything that is going to make the novice/medium aware of the "here and now" must be erased.

Regarding food prior, a heavy meal should be avoided, as it will make you feel uncomfortable, as should drinking alcohol or carbonated drinks. A light meal however is acceptable. I find it physiologically beneficial before going to any trance group/demonstration to have a shower prior. As mentioned this is purely from a psychological point of view as it helps me to mentally prepare. As always our own circumstances dictate.

You will already have gathered this group's aims are about helping one novice medium in his/her unfoldment. This method of sitting is more simplistic for the spirit people. Think of the power. If it is being divided between say 5 people over an hour each person will be allotted 20% and maximum time to work 10 minutes. If however that five were sitting for one then 100% of the power can be used in a 50-minute time span. Is it any wonder when people sit for each other the process is laboured? The "old fashioned" way of sitting for one novice works. When I raise this point students say to me "people won't sit for one"………………

I reply, "the right people will"!!

Of course you could extend the sitting period to 90 minutes and 2 novices could share the time (40 minutes each approx.). I still feel however sitting for the unfoldment of one person is preferable. Consider your sitters' attention span.

Having looked thus far at these aspects let us now discuss the practical. The following exercises have been practised over a number of years. They are not intended as being "laid in stone" but are given as suggestions to aid your unfoldment. Use your own sensitivity in application and don't be afraid to use your own individuality and awareness accordingly. Remember, your spirit is unique, work with the reality and celebrate that individualistic power.

Pearl of wisdom

"Remember, the pathway never ends"

CHAPTER 8

Exercises

This first exercise is aimed at a novice medium with a trained medium being their minder and sitters. This exercise is not suitable for everyone to use at the same time in a group or on an individual basis if you are still in a training circle. It can however be used for those of you who are not considered "novice" but still have trouble "letting go" whilst sitting on your own.

Exercise: Recognise and release
Suggested time 30 minutes

- Awareness of other people.
- Awareness of self.
- Passive mind.
- Awareness of one's own spirit power.
- Blending with your discarnate team.
- Being at one.

Sit in a chair that is supportive to your back. Close your eyes

If your mind is thinking in this reality of here and now you will not leave the beta state. So, rather than battle with the thinking process, deal with it and let go. Hence the heading "recognise and release" We start the process by recognising others and dismissing any physical distractions (1) **before** focus on self (2). If we go into our own sacred space first it will not have such an empowering effect, as we would leave the inner awareness (Alpha) then revisit Beta. You as the medium have to be master over mind and not allow mind to be master. Naturally until the process has been refined it will ebb and flow, so don't expect miracles in the early stages!!

When you have mentally withdrawn from the here and now, focus on the breath. Breathe in a manner, which is comfortable to you. Allow the breath to find its own rhythm. Don't force this, let it happen naturally. Your heart may be racing, slow this down with the breath and tell yourself "all is well" or other affirmation. It is normal in some people for this to occur. It's due to two reasons. One nerves and two the acceleration of the nervous system.

At this point use one of these affirmations to help you focus. I teach the following:

- My spirit no longer sleeps.
- All is well.
- I trust the supreme power.
- My mind is open to the Universe.

Alternatively ask your own spirit for an affirmation prior to sitting.

Then mentally **say,** physically **believe,** and spiritually **know.**

What are affirmations?
Statements of positive truth. By voicing the phrase we are mentally taking charge of our inner dialogue. By telling ourselves "my spirit no longer sleeps" (or other), we legitimise the statement that gives us a basis of belief.

In short affirmations can reinforce realities that we know but perhaps don't yet feel. Regular practice and dedication will lead us to that point. If using this process it will have three phases of:

Saying – Believing - Knowing.

When we merely say there is little emotion or feeling behind the expression. The second phase heightens this as our thought pattern changes and ultimately when we reach the third level experience has empowered us. It is a process that the majority of mediums encounter in their unfoldment.

The knowing creates a positive vibration for your team to begin to work with. You are becoming comfortable in your own sacred space and feeling a state of mental passivity (3). Your nervous system is becoming heightened and you may feel a mild tingling sensation through the spinal column or some other impressions on the physical body. Again recognise and release. Don't dwell in a feeling, live the experience. The power works on a very fast vibration so learn not to slow it down. Of course in the early stages you will slow it down as everything is new and we are our own worst enemy. The adage of "test ye the spirit" is important particularly at this level. Having a trained medium with you, he/she will not only add more power to the proceedings but also see through their own perception the unfoldment and be able to advise and assist you and your team accordingly. This medium is in effect "your guide" on the earth.

Now picture an elevator (4). Enter; close the doors press the level button you want to reach. The doors close and you feel very gently and slowly the elevator rising. When you have reached the suggested level the doors open and you walk into "light". The blending process takes place (5). Following which you are in the power. Any words or feelings expressed at this point (6).

Your circle leader will know when to get you to retrace the steps and talk you through the process. You should take time in this readjustment. If at any point your logical mind tries to dominate just bring the affirmation into the mind. This simple act brings focus and stimulates the emotional self and enables the subconscious to be alive being master over the consciousness.

Sitting physically on your own
If you have been sitting for a period of time and are aware of your helpers etc. use this exercise deleting awareness of others and replacing that aspect with the surroundings. It is still necessary you retrace your steps however to close the exercise. Simply to adjust your own awareness from the" inner "world to the physical reality. In both cases "walk back into life" when ready and in an alert state. Having a drink of water is a physical action that aids the process.

Please note: It is in order for you to sit on your own if you have been sitting for a period of time for this process. It is not advisable however for a novice medium to sit for the deeper entranced states without a trained medium with them. The reason? Firstly you need someone to give encouragement and guidance to you for the process to unfold. Secondly that person by their presence are giving extra power for the spirit people to work with and thirdly should any power manifest it would be of benefit to the sitters.

My caution is not because anything will possess you or you will lose control it's purely from an educational and fundamental perspective.

Second Exercise
Individual or group practice.

Suggested time 20 minutes.

Empowerment

Everyone exists on several levels of reality simultaneously – the physical, mental, emotional, and spiritual. We live with these on a daily basis without even realising.

When we meditate and attune with our own spirit self our consciousness is raised beyond physical restrictions. This exercise helps to examine our feelings beyond the five senses of sight, sound, touch, taste, and smell.

The process helps us to:
- Find inner strength.
- Realise we are not alone on our spiritual journey.
- Acknowledges our own spirit powers.

The spirit world has taught us for countless generations "our minds are the great architect of life". Consequently they can both build (positive) and destroy (negative). As we think we become. Already in your life this reality will have been realised. Please consider this and come to your own conclusions.

Empowerment
- Instils confidence.
- Aids spiritual awakening.
- Helps others by your example.

This is an excellent exercise for use in empowering your own spirit. If you are a novice trance medium, this exercise can be practised on your own. Alternatively if you just want to sit in the power of your spirit it is equally productive. It can also be used as a led meditation for a group.

Ensure you are not going to be disturbed. Sit in a chair, which is supportive to your back. Avoid low soft chairs or settees.

Close your eyes and be aware of the breath. Breathe in a manner, which is comfortable for you. Don't force, anticipate or create any stress in your thoughts or tension in the body. If there is any physical tension tell your body to relax. Begin to feel at peace. Be master over the mind and create a positive mental strength.

Tell yourself "my spirit no longer sleeps" follow the process through from saying/believing/knowing. You should feel a quickening within your sacred space.

When you are ready I want you to visualize yourself standing before the entrance of a walled garden. What season is it? How tall is the wall, what is the texture? Is there a gate/wooden door/archway/just an opening or something else between you and the garden? Find the image and study it for a while.

Now through the impression you can see glimpses of the garden, its power and spiritual essence is drawing you forward. Remember if at any time the mind wanders just focus on the affirmation "my spirit no longer sleeps"

Allow your imagination to be free, that's how your spirit communicates with you. We look upon the imagination as "the mirror of the mind"

Enter the garden and look around you. Using the sense of **SIGHT ONLY** what can you see? Is it a cottage garden laid out in a formal design or is it neglected? Are there any flowers? If so what are the colours? Are there any weeds or thistles growing between the flowers? Are there any fruit trees or vegetables? Keep focusing on the sight only - what can you see?

Using the sense of **SMELL** can you detect any fragrance from the flowers? If so breathe it in and feel a healing process within that power.

Using your sense of **TOUCH** pick up a handful of soil. Is it dry or lifeless or rich in nutrients? What do the flowers feel like to touch?

Using your sense of **HEARING** can you hear the birds singing? If not what can you hear?

Is there a breeze on your face? Is the sun shining? Is the sky overcast or clear? Look above you what can you **SEE** and **FEEL**? If you are by the sea can you **TASTE** the salt air?

Look at the wall that encloses the garden is it low, head height or imposing?

Are there any special features in your garden such as a sundial, raised bed of herbs, a pond or something else?

Now find somewhere to sit and contemplate your surroundings. Ask your spirit a question that is appertaining to your spiritual journey. Allow those returning thoughts to be free and enjoy this spiritual connection in your sanctuary that is beyond imagination.

When you feel the images/feelings are fading it is time to retrace your steps and bring your mind back to the waking consciousness

Guidelines

It is impossible to give a clear perspective on what each aspect of this exercise mean. You are going to have to come to your own conclusions. Every aspect will have a meaning in relevance to your spiritual growth and openness to listen. You see, we are all different and this must be taken into consideration during any unfoldment process. What you understand today changes as you evolve, that's why mediumship is a never-ending pathway of discovery. Have you found the more you learn the less you know? What a wonderful adventure!

This exercise will highlight which of your senses are dominant and which need working on.

Spirit told me recently "the more the medium becomes known in your world the more they become known in ours" Let us consider that for a moment. What were they actually saying? The level of success in achieving the process of communication and acting as that voice for the discarnate becomes stronger. As your confidence blossoms so does the trust. You become a clearer channel so those in the other world see your worth as a reliable, trustworthy worker. Perseverance and worth have been proven. We often talk about our need to trust but also look at this from the spirit world's perspective. They have to learn to trust us. How difficult that must be for them.

It is also advisable to keep a journal. Noting details of experience following each sitting. The process is as already stated very slow, by keeping a journal will give you a reminder on how far you have come. The mind has a way or recalling, "what is" as opposed to "what was". I tell students to "celebrate what they have achieved as opposed to being disappointed on what they didn't accomplish." Remember failure is an attitude not an outcome.

When a New York reporter asked Thomas Edison "Sir, how does it feel to have failed 699 times before your 700th attempt proved successful in the invention of the electric light?"

He replied, "I did not fail 699 times, I proved that those 699 times did not work".

That's the attitude to emulate.

Third exercise
SEE AND SENSE

Novice Medium

Trained medium

Sitters

Suggested time 30 minutes

During the induced state of entrancement the sitters and trained medium will make notes on what they perceive with the novice. Whist the novice is in the state of entrancement the sitters should not vocalise their perceptions. To do so would awaken the natural curiosity of the novice and not provide the right conditions. They must not pass notes to each other; the conditions must be uninterrupted to create the right results.

Under the direction of the trained medium when the novice has returned to the" waking state" the observations can be discussed.

It must be understood that any observations are based upon the individual's perception. Any statements as such must be examined with clarity and reason. Emotional sensationalism must be avoided. This is where the sensitivity of the trained medium is paramount.

When correctly applied this exercise keeps everyone involved and gives empowerment to the group core.

Fourth exercise
Suggested time 20 minutes.

The Bridge to Eternity
Suitable for individual use and also for group work.

Sit in a manner, which is comfortable to you, and use the breath as a focus.

When you feel at peace and have dealt with the usual distractions begin to build a bridge in your mind. It may be one you already know, seen a picture of or simply allow your imagination to create the image. Whichever methods you choose allow it to happen spontaneously.

Using your senses what can you see look at every aspect and examine the scenery. Take your time and enjoy the experience. Stimulate the other four senses in the exercise.

Eventually be aware of other powers on the opposite side of the bridge. These are your guides/helpers/loved ones. Extend your awareness into that communion. Now allow the spirit power to commune and relay whatever feelings/messages/inspiration etc.

Before the exercise concludes the spirit power will leave you a gift. It may be a word, object or feeling. You in turn will leave a gift for the spirit; again it may be a word object or feeling.

Take your mind back through the process and return to the full waking state.

This is a very good exercise if you are looking for some confirmation. Whatever you see/sense is of course personal to you. To get confirmation ask your spirit friends to validate some points either from the rostrum during a service/demonstration or if you have a private sitting. Many students have done this and their spirit team have co-operated. You see they will if we ask.

All these exercises bring a degree of focus with imaginative unfoldment. It seems a contradiction in terms when we speak of passivity and on the other hand are asking your mind to be somewhat active. However it is a step we must take on the pathway that will lead us to the required point of suggestion, inspired or otherwise. Eventually when we have worked through the layers of the mind we are clearer channels for our team to work with.

Fifth and Sixth exercises
Only suitable for circle supervision.

These two very simplistic exercises are offered as a means for encouraging speech. At the beginning the thoughts will be predominantly the novice medium's but regular use of this exercise will bring:

Focus for the medium.

A starting point for the inspirers.

Continual assessment to progress.

The tree of life
Sit in a manner, which is comfortable to you.

Your circle leader will have taken you into a degree of blending.

At this point your mind will be in a scramble, as previous sittings have not necessitated speech. Use the breath as a means of relaxation.

Begin by saying "I am the tree of life"…………….. Then allow the thoughts that enter your mind to be expressed. Don't try and make sense of what is being said just allow it to happen. Have the sessions recorded so afterwards you can listen to them and over a period of time you should see a difference in:

Speech patterns and phraseology

Emphasis and flow of inspiration

The sixth exercise is called

I have come to say
Adopt the same principle as previous exercise.

I would only recommend this exercise to the novice who has been sitting over a period of time and has mastered the previous exercise. It requires a very strong degree of trust, which can only come over a period of time of sitting and blending with your team.

When you feel settled in your "sacred space" begin by saying "I have come to say"......you won't have a clue what it is, but by allowing the positive statement to be expressed you are giving your team the opportunity to work with you in a very free manner. You will not have any prepared script in your mind and as previously just allow it to happen.

Before speech can be enacted you will already have studied the layers of the mind and will be discerning with your unfoldment. This will be on going as there is no such thing as a fully developed medium. You must always be discerning and follow what you feel in the process. I know I keep talking about time and patience but that is the core issue behind all spiritual endeavours.

Remember if a house is built on quick sand it will not stand the test of time. If it is built on a firm foundation then it will.

Any form of mediumship requires a lifetime of dedication commitment and service. There is no other way for the true progression of spiritual mediumship. That is the foundation, which the great mediums of the past built their power upon. It worked for them, I have adopted the same principle and the door is now open for you.

Seventh Exercise
Only suitable for experienced Novices

The previous exercises have been allowing you to actively stimulate the mind in co-operation with your spirit and higher powers. This exercise is completely passive, and should be done on a daily basis for about a 20 minute duration. The sitting time should always be the same as it is an appointment with your spirit team.

Be Still
Focus on the breath and bring the affirmation into your mind "Be still". Keep repeating this affirmation until you feel peaceful and calm. A sense of detachment will eventually be felt - it may take several sessions to accomplish. So don't expect miracles on the first sitting.

Allow the spirit within you to influence the experience. You are no longer stimulating through your physical senses, but are allowing the spirit essence of you to come to the fore. It is this feeling that will blend with your team in the spirit world.

How do we know?
- The sensations will have more clarity.
- The sitting experience will be even more positive.
- You will notice a difference in your interaction with others.
- Life will take on a different perspective.

- The power will not be vague and spasmodic but structured with a purpose.
- If the above aspects are not realised then you are obviously not ready for this exercise.
- So go back and look at your reasons and circumstances. There you will find the answer.

Trance and Colour

Eighth exercise

1. Breathe in Red and Orange at the same time into the solar plexus.

2. Breathe in yellow into the heart centre.

3. Breathe in blue into the brow centre.

4. Fill body and surround yourself with all colours of the spectrum.

5. Reach out to the spirit world.

This exercise was given by Minister Gordon Higginson, past President of "The Spiritualists' National Union" and Principal of "The Arthur Findlay College"

When working with this exercise take your time. As with any exercise it gives the novice medium a focus and stops the overactive imagination. It stimulates the centres of power thus enabling a blending process.

If you feel impressed you can change the colours as you work with the exercise over a period of time.

Pearl of wisdom
"Time is your friend"

CHAPTER 9

Points to Ponder

To cultivate inner awareness is not enough. The pathway you are investigating is never ending and we are on a journey of discovery. History has shown that you don't have to be spiritual to be a medium, but I feel it helps if you are. None of us are perfect, if we were we would not be on this journey and neither would our inspirers!

Over the years I have had to work on:

Faith
I don't mean this in any subservient manner; I refer to a faith based on knowledge and reason.

Courage
Believing in you.

Individuality
Loving you for who and not what you are.

Balance
Between body/mind and spirit.

Judgement
Keep your own counsel.

Perfection
Look to yourself not others.

Structure
But still be flexible.

Hope
All things are possible.

Tolerance
With self and others.

Understanding

Living with simplicity.

There are many other aspects, which are still being discovered on a daily basis.

I was told some time ago that we come into this world with "life's lessons" and once learnt another would come along. Have you noticed a pattern in your life? Only one day to realise enough is enough? Then embracing the lesson and moving forward.

Our mediumship does not offer us all the answers but if we really allow it to spiritualise our being then real progress can be made. The key however is within us. That's why daily contemplation is extremely important and like some of the people surveyed from Harvard (see meditation) it will become as natural to us a breathing.

I look at unfoldment like the chrysalis and the butterfly. Nothing can be forced. If it is the butterfly does not emerge in its perfect state.

I don't take credit for the following piece of inspiration it was e-mailed to me some time ago. The author is unknown.

One day a small opening appeared in a chrysalis. A man sat and watched for several hours as a butterfly struggled to force its way through the little hole. Then the butterfly seemed to stop making any progress. It appeared it had developed as far as it could and was unable to evolve further.

So the man decided to help the butterfly, he took a pair of scissors and snipped off the remaining bit of the chrysalis. The butterfly then emerged easily. It had a swollen body and small-shrivelled wings. The man continued to watch the butterfly because he expected at any moment, the wings would enlarge and expand to be able to support the body, which would contract in time. Neither happened; in fact, the butterfly spent the rest of its life crawling around with a swollen body and shrivelled wings. It was never able to fly.

Acting in kindness and haste, the man did not understand that because the chrysalis was restrictive it required more of a struggle for the butterfly to get through the tiny opening. This is Gods way of forcing the fluid from the body of the butterfly and its wings so that it would be ready for flight once it achieved its freedom from the origin. Sometimes struggles are exactly what we need in our life. If God allowed us to go through life without any struggles it would cripple us. We would not be as strong as we are, or what we could have been.

I asked for strength...
God gave me difficulties to make me strong.
I asked for wisdom...
God gave me problems to solve.
I asked for prosperity..
And God gave me brain and brawn to work.
I asked for courage..
And God gave me danger to overcome.
I asked for love..
And God gave me troubled people to help.
I asked for favours..
And God gave me opportunities.
I received nothing I asked for,
I received everything I needed.

It's of no benefit if we make giant leaps along the way; if we do we have missed many points of progress. Baby steps are far more productive. If we fall down that's ok, provided we stand up again and not wallow in self – pity or bruised pride.

As a sensitive of course we feel things so much more intently because that part of us is awakened. Our imaginations in many cases are "over – active", they have to be to enable to spirit people to impress us. Time and patience in this way of life have led me not to believe these points but know them as a living realty. You of course may disagree and that quite rightly is your choice.

Mediumship is far more than sitting and blending. It's a way of life. We are living two realities and at times it can be difficult to focus on that which is mundane. In the physical world we need rules and regulations, as it is necessary to uphold some semblance of order. If we are involved with any "spiritual organisation" it is also important to have a framework of ideals and obligations to work with. At times however to the medium this can impinge their natural flow of power. From a personal perspective if I am asked to do a specific job I do it. To wait for a committee meeting or put the inspiration through a procedure that is outside that ideal for me does not work. I have been involved with committees in the past and it was right for that moment. I have since learned as the sensitivity has grown the pathway of administration requires a different mode of thinking. Thank God for administrators who administer, mediums that minister and spirit both incarnate and discarnate which inspire us all.

Pearl of wisdom
> *"You are amazing, so always be amazed"*

CHAPTER 10

Closing Thoughts

Here is a sample of some questions, which have been asked over a period of time whilst in the various stages of entrancement.

Question
In your talk this evening you mentioned returning again, are you suggesting there is such a thing as reincarnation?

Answer
Reincarnation is a fact. How can any soul learn it's lessons in three score years and ten? Many of course do not even reach this goal for various reasons.

Do not look at what you represent today but at the totality of your soul. the spirit, which inhabits your physical body, is an aspect of that life's breath. That divine spark has chosen along with other minds to fulfil whatever destiny is required for its progression. You see, you are never alone, how can you be for you are spirit. So when death of that body beckons the aspect returns to the source. Because of procreation other lives will be born and the genetic trace continues. How often has it been said that a death is followed by a birth?

I cannot say precisely what length of time is required for such an act, for it requires great planning and organisation. It is an extremely complicated process but nevertheless a reality for those who are ready and willing to return to the physical experience of life. If the soul is not willing then it will not happen. Free will is as applicable here as it is on your plain of reality.

We do understand the difficulty some people have comprehending this truth because of limited knowledge they are only able to grasp half its value.

Consider the man who learns different languages. He goes to school, is shown and taught the method of articulation. It is not until he lives in the country however that he fully understands the language and true depth behind the words. So it is with your question and many others who aspire to understand.

Question
There was recently a probe, which landed on Titan. My Son wanted to know would we find other life there or on any other planet. If so would we recognise them as such?

Answer
Your Son has a very inquiring and intelligent mind, which is good in one so young.

Where there is a purpose there is life but because of the limitations of the physical senses people incarnate perceive all as equals of expression. This is not so. No planet is dead to life for it is part of its purpose to create a living environment for evolution. In certain cases we use these places for experimental reasons but not as you would perceive in the form you exist now. Planet Earth does not have priority of expression; the Universe is a vast vortex of power.

It remains a mystery to us as to why mankind is intent on finding out about other planets when it is very clear he cannot cope with understanding the mechanics of Earth. Such is the complexity of Man.

Tell your Son there are other expressions of life but not to imagine them to be personalities of destruction or indeed in the human form. They are not in that form because the atmosphere would not be possible for such activity.

Question
I know we have a doorkeeper or someone that looks after us. Do we keep the same one or do they change throughout our lifetime?

Answer
Prior to incarnation there will be one who has said they will accompany you for whatever purpose. That one will be the main source between your spirit and the divine source. They will however be part of another group where minds will be inspiring them to help you along the pathway. We do not always succeed as we would have hoped but nothing is lost in the experience of trying. There have been times in your life when "higher powers" have been required; it is then your doorkeeper has sought guidance. Remember they are not the fountains of all knowledge, far from it. Is not a drop of water a part of the Ocean? Consequently as a drop of water the doorkeeper has the Ocean to call upon when your tide of life has been difficult.

Question
What happens to souls upon transition that haves committed atrocities whilst upon the earth?

Answer
As Spirit you have light and dark within you. How you manifest these powers whilst incarnate depends upon your desire. Heaven and Hell are states of mind and it is what is created that transmutes into an experience. If the individual is so entrenched in their way of life a blanket of fog is created in the auric field, which is extremely difficult for us to penetrate. It is like a wall. We try to inspire other minds to help that one "see the light" as their

minds are more penetrable. We are on hand to help others who are victims of such atrocities.

When the personality comes into our dimension they are shown they pathway they have trod. The blanket I spoke of will have had an effect upon their spirit and until they accept responsibility for those actions they will be encased in that blanket. Each case is individual and as such requires particular attention. True progression can only be attained when the injustice has been replaced by kindness. The soul can still be deluded it is therefore of paramount importance for true progression it is not.

As to those souls who were victims and have crossed the great divide, many choose to confront their perpetrator and if possible ways are provided for such opportunities. I must emphasise however that at no point does any spirit sit in judgement on another, on the contrary. Tolerance and understanding are powers far beyond that of anger. Lessons are learned and in time what was an injustice becomes a light for others to learn from.

Question
What thoughts can you enlighten us with regarding the changes that are occurring on Mother Earth?

Answer
Your question refers to the climate changes, which the physical world is experiencing as a result of mankind robbing the planet of its life breath. You see where there is a cause there has to be an effect. That is natural law in operation. It highlights the tremendous responsibility each person as a custodian of the earth. We have been trying to inspire minds for countless generations; often those individuals have been ridiculed for the seemingly madcap ideas they voiced. Consequently man has been like the

Ostrich and put his head in the sand. Mankind thinking he is superior over nature but in fact he is part of it.

Now you are seeing those results and people are experiencing hardships and difficulties because of past deeds of misguided greed and avarice at the expense of the planet. Yes the planet is retaliating and finally mankind is beginning to listen. It may seem harsh to the uninitiated but it is the only way the planet can begin to restore its balance and nourishment. When you are seriously ill treatment is required to aid your betterment and sometimes the condition becomes acute before any success. So it is with your question.

It is our earnest desire that mankind will continue to listen to reason and learn from past mistakes. Souls are now being born into matter to help in this process. Our aim is to safeguard the planet but as always we need co-operation from all concerned. It begins and ends with you. The responsibility is immense but it is all part of another aspect which is within the soul.

Question
Where exactly is the spirit world?

Answer
Your question suggests an understanding of a place as opposed to a state of mind.

Consider, you have an atlas in front of you. It tells your intelligence where the different countries are and if you avail yourself to the various means of technology available to you this can be proven. There are also places, which are still being discovered and as yet are not on your atlas because of progression.

When you sit in the power of your own spirit your awareness transcends the physicality of your surroundings and your mind state changes because of the vibrations created. The place you call the spirit world does not exist in an atlas because it is within you. Where you are there is spirit because you are spirit as I have said on many other occasions. So do not think as this as a country or continent, somewhere in the sky or depth of the earth. It is quite simply within you. At the point of physical death the vibration changes again and the spirit is reborn into a world that you recognised when you closed your physical eyes. It is then and only then the situation is reversed and we say where is the physical world, which I was part of ? Like you we are shown various methods to commune and acclimatise ourselves accordingly.

Question
What happens to our beloved pets when they go to spirit?

Answer
Within all life there is a spiritual expression. Your beloved pets have taught you many things whilst incarnate and you them. They were there to greet you irrespective of your moods or temperament and as such shared in the tapestry of your existence. The life span of domestic pets is not as humans because of the implications of unconditional love. If it were so then the impact and value of companionship would not be so enriching in your life.

As such that spiritual expression is released upon physical death and like you on transition will gravitate to a point where they are comfortable. There will be others who will who will have them in your charge, only for a period of time however , until you join them.

Love is not about separation it knows that one day that bonds that were in physical existence are fused again. Out of sight is never out of mind wherever the spirit may be. Reunion is a reality not a vague promise based on a religious belief.

Question
I have had four consecutive miscarriages. It was not until my fifth pregnancy that I was able to go full term. The Dr's could not give me any medical reason for this, can you?

Answer
This is a very sensitive question and I would first like to thank you for having the courage to speak publicly on this issue.

As free will is applicable whilst incarnate so it is in this dimension you call the spirit world. The medical profession were unable to find any physical reason for your miscarriages because there were none. The free will I spoke of was being utilised by the given spirit. Whilst this caused you as a parent and your family great distress over a time span your child has grown into a very sensitive adult and is working in the medical profession. There are no coincidences. I cannot say it was necessary for the series of events that touched your life to be part of this intended birth but they were utilised accordingly for everyone's betterment. Out of dismay springs hope. Your daughter brings that element to those she touches.

* The sitter confirmed later her daughter was a Dr and the answer confirmed her own belief *

When questions are invited, and I can only speak from personal experience, my own curiosity can come to the surface. This is where the discipline of self has to be mastered and allow those working with me to share **their thoughts** with the sitter. That power already understands the needs of the individual and will couch the words according to the sitters own understanding. If I as the trance medium interfere in the process then the work will be clouded and not as pure. This is why when demonstrating the various stages, a trance medium will sometimes feel a stronger degree of hold than other occasions. The understanding of those observing also has to be taken into consideration. All thought creates an atmosphere and that in turn is an aspect which the spirit people work with during the demonstration. So the outcome does not solely lie on the shoulders of the medium but all present. The pure intention is paramount in the objective.

I wish you well on your pathway and conclude with this piece of inspiration that was dictated to me some time ago from my team. I have found it to be a solid foundation of understanding over the years and I offer it to you as food for thought.

INTENT

We are one.

At times I reach through the depths of your mind and for
me
it is a source of inspiration
a reflection of God's plan.
I can awaken a power, which is yours, because I am Not
just within you but are the totality of you.
I am not a stranger on some far distant shore: I live within
your
being and I am a constant companion within the
expression of life.

We are one.

Boundaries are laid by your lack of vision: perfection is
impossible once imperfection is embraced.
When you allow me to I can speak through your voice,
stimulating a purpose, which is ours.
United in service a beacon of hope can touch others.

We are one.

Be not afraid, for fear can create a lodgement within your
being
It disables and detaches the source of all life.
Be still and feel my essence within the stillness.
Invite the power of knowing into self, for that is where I
reside.

We are one.

I have no nationality, religious doctrine or hidden agenda
Together we share the joys and sorrows of experience.
Allow peace to be your garment and radiance its weave.
Yes at times this will vary for such is progression
when carved within the Soul.
I ask you always to remember

We are one.

Given through inspiration.

FURTHER SUGGESTED READING AND CONTACTS

*The University of Spiritualism by Harry Boddington.

*The Philosophy of SNU Spiritualism.

*Red Cloud speaks. Estelle Roberts.

*Philosophy of Silver Birch. (various)

*On the side on angels. By Minister Jean Basset.

*Living in two worlds. Autobiography Ursula Roberts.

*Teachings of Ramadahn. (various)

*This is Spiritualism Maurice Barbanell.

*All of the above obtainable Arthur Findlay College www.arthurfindlaycollege.org

SDU Publications www.s-upton.com Spiritualists' Classics

Matthew's CD Embracing the Spirit.

A practical approach to meditation and attunement. www.ministermatthewsmith.co.uk

CD Lecture Evidential Mediumship. Guidance and techniques for the discerning medium Available through web site pay/pal facility.

Residential Courses

SPIRITUS Residential day courses around the UK.

See www.ministermatthewsmith.co.uk

Arthur Findlay College

www.arthurfindlaycollege.org

Arthur Findlay College Stansted Hall Essex. UK CM24 8UD.

For the advancement of Psychic Science. Tel: 01279 813636

Spiritualists' National Union - www.snu.org.uk

Redwoods Stansted Hall Essex UK CM24 8UD Tel: 01279 816363

To promote the advancement and diffusion of knowledge of the religion and religious philosophy/science of Spiritualism as based upon the Seven Principles of National Spiritualism.